Personal Finance and Wealth Creation Secrets

Mastering the Game of Money

By: Alan Eduardo

Foreword By: Raymond Aaron

New York Times Best-Selling Author

LEGAL DISCLAIMER

The information provided within this book is for general informational purposes only. While we try to keep the information up-to-date and correct, there are no representations or warranties, express or implied, about the completeness, accuracy, reliability, suitability or availability with respect to the information, products, services, or related graphics contained in this book or websites for any purpose. Any use of this information is at your own risk.

The information is not advice, and should not be treated as such. This book is provided "as is" Alan Eduardo Ortega makes no representations or warranties in relation to the legal information on this book.

No part of this Book may be reproduced or transmitted in any form or by any means, electronic or mechanical, including photocopying, recording or by any information storage and retrieval system, without written permission from the author.

The author has made every effort to ensure the accuracy of the information within this book was correct at time of publication. The author does not assume and hereby disclaims any liability to any party for any loss, damage, or disruption caused by errors or omissions, whether such errors or omissions result from accident, negligence, or any other cause.

This book is not intended to provide personalized legal, accounting, financial, or investment advice. Readers are encouraged to seek the counsel of competent professional with regard to such matters as interpretation of the law, proper accounting procedures, financial planning and investment strategies. The Author and Publisher specifically disclaim any liability, loss or risk which is incurred as consequence, directly or indirectly of the use and application of any of the contents of this work.

Personal Finance and Wealth Creation Secrets. Copyright © 2016 by Alan Eduardo Ortega. All rights are reserved. Printed in the United

States of America. No part of this book may be used or reproduced in any manner whatsoever without written permission of the author.

ISBN: 978-1530443925

<u>DEDICATION</u>

This book is dedicated to my family, friends, every person that bought this book or is reading this book, thanks to all my mentors, my clients, and the people that have believed in me, especially to the people whose lifes will be changed and transformed for reading this book.

Alan Eduardo

TESTIMONIALS

I thank Alan for all the support, for guiding me on my investments, for coaching me and to be the best business partner I ever had; thank you Alan.

Samuel Rojas

Since the first time I spoke with him, I knew he was the real deal. I like his ideas and ways of thinking – very energetic, great investor, very positive. Thank you, Alan, for helping me with my investments.

Louis John

Alan is a great guy. He has helped me with my real estate deals. He is a great investor. Thank you for all the support and wisdom; thanks for helping out.

Camilo Palacio

This book will give you some good ideas to get ahead financially, good tips, good advice. I have learned a lot with Alan and you will too.

Sandra Ramirez

TABLE OF CONTENTS

Chapter 1: Spiritual Wealth

- God and Wealth
- You are Already Wealthy
- Planting The Seed
- Knowledge and Faith (2 Powerful Strengths)

Chapter 2: Personal Finance

- Personal Finance
- Financial Literacy
- Managing your Budget
- He looks Rich, but he Isn't

Chapter 3: Money Management

- From 55K to 6k with No Girl, No House
- Saving Plan
- Basic of Accounting

Chapter 4: The Smart way to pay high interest

- Don't Get Debt you Don't Need
- Transferring Your Credit Cards Balance
- Avoid Parkinson's law
- Be Your Own Debt Settlement

- Get Educated
- Don't Cut Your Credit Cards
- Always Pay More for Principal

Chapter 5: Wealth Creation

- The law of abundance
- Powerful Leverage
- Mentors, Role Models, or Coaches
- Priorities – your Goals
- The Rule of 72
- Monopoly, Mastering the Game of Money
- Albert Einstein & Napoleon Hill's Philosophy

Chapter 6: The 3 Pillars of Wealth

- Real Estate Investing
- Stocks, Forex
- Businesses "Online Business"
- The Market Place

Chapter 7: Protect Yourself and Your Assets

- Insurance
- Asset Protection
- Final Words

ACKNOWLEDGMENTS

I am grateful to my creator and to the many people who have blessed my life and inspired me beyond words. I am truly grateful for their love, friendship, encouragement, and support, most important my dear mother, Carmen Tornyai. Her patience and trust in me is eternal and cherished. To my brothers, Gianni and Carlitos, who are an inspiration in my life and my sister, Carmen, whom I adore – thank you for being there. I want to thank Valeria Bejar and family, Rinaldo Garcia, Martha Yera, Manolo Yera, Manolito Yera, Aida Clark and her husband Justin Clark, Samuel Rojas, Katia Rojas & The KSR Team, Victoria Achamizo, Anna trishch, Emiliano Espinosa, Sandra Ramirez, Mario Zamarripa and his wife Miriam, Hortencia Calderon, Danny and the entire Property Management Advisors team. Jennifer Gia for being an amazing realtor, my friend Mike Viera another amazing realtor, Marko Rubel, Nijaz Durmic, Gary Hardee, Tatiana Ferrigno and husband John, Tony Mesa, Victor Ponce, Vick Strazeurs for teaching me all of his techniques in High Traffic Academy, Lee McIntyre, Anik Singal, Bob Proctor, Robert Allen and the entire team in Wealth Enlighten Institude , Robert Kiyosaki, Mark Victor Hanson, Russ Dalbey, Terry Hale, Cherif Medawar, the Founder of The Institute of Commercial Real Estate and the entire team, The Entire staff teachers and workers of New Professions Technical Institute, Market Traders Institute and the entire team. The entire staff of Trump University and all the coaches, Raymond Aaron, Brian Tracy for teaching me the psychology of achievement, John Maxwell, Adam Markel CEO of New Peaks, T. Harv Eker and the entire MMI Team. Robert Riopel, Andres Hurtado, Monica Main, Felipe Orellana, Luis Aguilar, Joaquin Orellana, Gerry Villegas, Jose Fernandez, Luis Alcala for being good friends, Gratitude Training and the entire staff. Christine Bascon, Sandra Apan, Miguel Martin, Gemma Romaguera, Dorothy Allen, Louis John, Camilo Palacio, Gayle Bertsch, and Sebastian Apelbaum.

FOREWORD

I AM EXTREMELY impressed with Alan Eduardo Ortega high level of education in finance and investments. After reading this powerful book, I saw his expertise level and willingness to help people; I recommend it as a must read! I feel this book should be mandatory reading for anyone who wants to master their finances and create wealth. What makes this book so fascinating is that it explains all the details about money management and the three pillars of wealth. Take this journey by reading this book. It will dramatically increase your financial IQ and show you how to be smarter with your money. This book contains strategies and techniques about wealth creation techniques that you can use in your life to improve your finances.

RAYMOND AARON

New York Times Best-Selling Author

CHAPTER 1

SPIRITUAL WEALTH

God and Wealth

This chapter is not about religion. You can be very spiritual and be very wealthy; they are not mutually exclusive. The idea is to shine everywhere you go, whether you are an employee, self-employed, a business owner, or investor.

Let's start by saying that wealth could mean a lot of things to different people; we have different opinions, different beliefs and a lot of people have their own interpretation about wealth. But God is NOT against wealth or abundance at all. God is abundance; he wants you to be happy in abundance, have joy in abundance, amazing relationships, and have all the great things you want in abundance. But you have to believe it and help yourself. You have to create it for yourself, just like God created the earth. The Bible says that you are created at the image of your creator, that means we can create just like God did or just like Larry Page and Sergey Brin created Google, like Mark Zuckerberg created Facebook. Just like Donald Trump can create buildings, like I created this book. Just like Henry Ford created Ford Automobiles, you can create as well. You can create or buy good investments, you can create or buy good businesses; you can create a big fat account if you want to. The only thing that is stopping you is your own belief.

If God is the creator of all things, He knows which stock is going to go up or down, what will be the next billion dollar idea, the best real estate deal in your market. Why not have the creator of all things as a partner? You can have the wealthiest partner in the world, the one who knows everything.

God sees you wealthy already; he wants you to be extremely wealthy. Here are some people in history that were servants of God who had extreme wealth.

King David was wealthy. **King Solomon** was greater in riches and wisdom than all the other kings of the earth.

Abraham, the father of faith, was extremely rich. Abraham was very rich in cattle, in silver, and in gold.

Joseph, Isaac, and Job were righteous man blessed by God with a wealth of possessions.

Moses. Even when he was born in poverty, he was rich spiritually. There was no material wealth that could compare to the spiritual wealth he had, and all the miracles he had done, even the wealthy people in that time wish they had his power. Everything starts within. True wealth starts within us.

Jesus was poor in material wealth, but he was spiritually wealthy, talking about God and God is abundance, the kingdom of God, heaven, peace, love, patience, glory, and righteousness, people would call him the King of the Jews, others will say he was the king of kings.

You Are Already Wealthy

The Bible said that the kingdom of God is within us; everything starts within us. There is no kingdom on earth that compares to that, there is no building that compares to that no diamond or material thing can compare to God and your spirit, there is power in you and a lot more than you can imagine

Where God is, there is abundance and God is in you.

God wants you to possess wealth in abundance but it all starts by having faith. Look deep inside you and start shining with your thoughts and spirit.

If you have a great wife or husband, consider yourself wealthy. If you have great kids, consider yourself wealthy. If you have great brothers and sisters, consider yourself wealthy. If you have a great mom like the one I have, consider yourself wealthy. If you have health, consider yourself wealthy and even if you don't have health right now, still consider yourself wealthy. If you are a believer of God, you are already wealthy. It doesn't matter what position you are at right now; if you are reading this book, you should consider yourself wealthy and believe you are going to possess more wealth.

I am not a father yet, but I do know that having a son or daughter is the biggest thing that could happen to anyone. I could tell just by looking at my friends that are parents, my brothers, my aunt, and cousins how they love their kids there is no material wealth that could buy that, they are already wealthy in their spirit and in their heart. They have their own treasure and that is priceless. It is the same way God looks at us; we are his treasure and that is priceless.

Planting the Seed

Plant the seed and let it grow, ask God for wisdom and he will give you wisdom. He will show you the way and guide you through; remember true wealth is in the mind true wealth is in the spirit but first you need to plant the seed.

You can have a successful money tree in your life but you need to plant and believe that is going to grow in abundance. Knowing where to plant is very important if you plant in concrete or in a desert is not going to grow, the same way is with money.

If you are persistent with your goals, you will achieve them. That's why Proverbs 21:21 says whoever pursues righteousness and love finds life, prosperity, and honor. That means that you need to plant the seed. Believe and pursue your goals, pursue righteousness.

Don't treat your spirit with a poor mentality. Instead treat it with the mind of success, victory, glory, righteousness, and truth.

Please delete the seed of poor mentality; cut that tree right away. Delete the seed, delete that tree of bad habits, and replace it with good habits

Plant the Seed of greatness in your spirit, in your soul, in your heart, in your personality, and in your character.

Knowledge and Faith

Knowledge and faith will move mountains. According to science and research we only use 6% of our brain capacity others say that we use less than that. We can build building, walk on the moon, heal someone from a tumor, cancer and we are only using less than 6%. Some can heal with spiritual power, others as a doctor, imaging if we can use 100% all the time every single day. I don't believe in limitations. The sky is not the limit, nor the moon, not even this universe, I believe anyone can double, triple, and quadruple their income if they wanted to all they need to do is get the knowledge and act in faith, that faith will break any barrier or any obstacles. If they want to make 1 million dollar they can do it, 10 million, 100 million, 1 Billion, 10 Billion, 100 Billion, and more, I believe everything is possible. The Bible says if you believe all things are possible, all things not a few things but all things if that is true I don't know why people limit themselves or doubt.

John 14:12 Jesus says to John, "I very truly tell you, whoever believes in me will do the works I have been doing and they will do even greater things than these."

Do you think it is possible to do greater things than Jesus did? I know it is possible, I KNOW FOR A FACT it is possible.

But enough with Jesus. Do you think is possible to make $100,000 a year? A lot of people don't think they can; they think it is too much and too hard. They think somebody else could, but they can't. They limit themselves in their beliefs and that's the reason they will never make it. The answer is yes you can and you can add 2 or 3 zeros to that if you want.

Get the knowledge on investing. Learn where to plant your seed. Let this book be the beginning of your journey. Remember it all starts within, then learn to manage your own personal finance and find ways to create wealth. Creating wealth is not a secret. This is available to anyone and it is possible for you.

CHAPTER 2

PERSONAL FINANCE

Personal Finance is a broad subject. It consists of having the right mindset, the right education, behavior, and practices to control your finances.

The difference between the wealthy and everyone else consists of two things.

1. The wealthy know how to manage their money very well.

2. They know where to put that money so it can work for them.

To do this, they need to have the right knowledge first—knowing how to manage their money and knowing where to put it so it can grow, where to invest it in stocks, real estate in businesses etc…

At the end, it all comes down to improving your finances, managing it well, and improving your wealth. Half of this book will be about developing the right mindset for managing your money, your own personal finance, budgeting, savings, and lowering expenses and debt. The other half of this book will be about creating wealth. You are going to get some amazing tips on wealth creation and the three pillars of wealth—Real Estate Investing, Businesses, and Stocks.

With the right mindset, you will be able to see more opportunities; you will see more open doors. But even when you have the right mindset, you want to continue with your education to learn and grow, learn about financial literacy, maximize your wealth, and value of money throughout your life.

These practices start when you're a kid, since the first time you had money even if it was pennies in your pocket or a few dollars. Maybe your parents gave you an allowance or you earned your money by cutting the grass or washing the car. The question is how are you going to spend it. If you spend everything you make, soon you won't have much for the future, and that is something that parents need to teach their kids. The day people understand the importance of managing their own wealth correctly and investing correctly, the ride towards financial freedom would start.

Financial Literacy

Improve your financial future by improving your financial literacy if you want to be financially independent or become rich you need to learn and master financially literacy, this entire book is about improving your financial literacy. The key is to develop the right mindset to manage your money, create wealth, and hold on to your wealth.

If your investments or business create more money than your expenses without you having to work, you have reach financial independence. The idea is to enjoy the journey along the way and create wealth without the usual stress and struggle. These next chapters are going to help you move ahead in life and give you a better understanding of a wide range of personal finance topics.

Even if you work every day to get a paycheck, this book will help you and guide you to create more wealth and anyone can apply it regardless of their financial situation.

Improving your financial situation is a good thing to do at any time of the year. Many people find it easier at the beginning of a new year. Regardless of when you begin, the basics remain the same—the idea is to start now.

Managing Your Budget

There are different types of budgeting. We have the USA Budget, Corporate budget, small business budget, family budget, personal budget etc... The goal is to manage your money correctly to lower your expenses and liabilities. I know nobody likes the word *budget*, but is very important especially if you are just starting out. Be wise with your money it can make you a real fortune.

You might be surprised at how much money you can save each month just by looking at your regular spending. The reality is that most of us waste 12% to 35% of our income each month on things that don't really matter. From desire purchases to the careless way that we use electricity, there is a good chance you are not budgeting your money correctly. But if you did, you will have bigger savings and be able to put that money to work for you to put it to good use, instead of you working hard you will have your money working hard for you.

Start by looking to reduce your utility bills and other monthly bills. Think about your energy use and your water use to figure out ways to save money on your electricity bill, gas bill and water bill. Two other services that have many opportunities to cut back include the cable bill and cell phone bill. Reducing these five bills could easily save you over $200 a month and more, an average of $2,400 to $3,800 in a year. That's not too much at all, but if you put that money in a place where you can make 10% to 35% in compound interest, it will add up really fast and it will double and triple your money in no time and if every year you add up another $2,400. And this is just an example of a lower income family, this along will be enough to make them financially independent in the long run.

The main goal is to have control of your money instead of having your money controlling you, let's look at how to save money each month by reducing other expenses. Think ways that you can save money on groceries or save money on any other bills that are not necessary. Think about which payment you can cancel, as well as other playful spending that might not be necessary. These monthly costs might be stopping you from creating your true wealth.

Finally, look at some of your biggest monthly expenses. Look at your bank account often. I do it all the time. If you cannot do it every day, look at it at least three or four times a week. Look at your Bank Statement for the entire month and ask yourself how can I lower some expenses and liabilities that I don't need?

One day I got good advice from a multi-millionaire. He said if you don't have the discipline to save 2 cents, you are not going to save more when you get more. When he said that, I thought he was cheap. But then he said the same way people throw away 2 cents is the same way they throw away $2 and the same way they throw away $20 and in 1 year they would throw away over $2,000 easily, some between $2,000 to $20,000 and they don't even make a $40,000 income a year and then they wonder where the money went. How you do anything is how you do everything, and it is true in a way because the more money people make the more money they would spend in liabilities, except for those who become extremely wealthy or rich and this is an advice of someone who donated 8 million dollars when the economy was bad, do you think he knows something about money? I think he does. The same advice I got is the same advice I am telling you now. Don't get me wrong, pay yourself first, have fun but don't spend it all; don't spend everything you make and don't do it in credit either.

You may save money each month by refinancing your home as well so that you have a lower finance payment and lower interest but that is NOT always the case sometimes it could be greater amount you always wants to find out with your mortgage broker or the bank that gave you the loan or different banks. Just ask how much it would cost to refinance, that you want to know all the hidden fees and interest, for a short term and long term mortgage loan if it doesn't make sense don't do it, if you are going to do it make sure you have a plan. Don't put your equity in risk unless you are going to buy another house with equity or another good investment.

It's also possible to save by shopping around for better insurance rates. Whether its auto insurance or home insurance, you can save big each year by getting the best premium or just by asking for a discount, remember this always ask for special promotions or discounts, don't be scare of asking just ask who knows sometimes you will get some special deals, all you have to do is ask specially if you are going to buy a car, a house, or insurance just ask for a discount, ask to get lower interest rate don't accept everything they give you, I know it may sound silly or weird but It can save you money in the long run. Do it as if you are negotiating, because that's what you are doing remember you want a good fair deal. Whether is a small deal or a big deal ask and lower all your debt, expenses, liabilities and interest rate get a good deal.

People that look rich but don't manage it well may end up broke again

In life, it is important to be responsible with your money whether you have $100 or millions of dollars. The idea is to be responsible and make smart financial decisions that make sense, but a lot of people don't have common sense. I have seen a lot of people who look rich or extremely wealthy but they are not. Let me give you an example of a guy who was self-employed—he was his own boss. He was making a nice income, he had a big house—a big debt worth about $1,000,000—a nice Porsche (in credit), and his wife had a nice BMW (in credit). They also had two more cars in credit and a boat in credit. But in 2008/2009, the economy went down in flames. He couldn't make payments on the property and he was facing foreclosure. His self-employed business wasn't doing to good, he had a lot of credit card debt and then one day he saw one of my signs. He gave me a call and told me his story.

I decided to help him, but there was a huge problem. He had a 30-day notice saying that the bank was going to take away his house. He showed me all the legal papers, First Mortgage, Second Mortgage, and all his financials to see if I could do something to help him. He was behind on payments by more than a year; he owed about one million, but the property was only worth $620,000. He owed money on all his cars, boat, and huge credit card debt. He waited until the last moment to call me. He should have called me long time ago, but that's okay.

Now why am I telling you this story? The reason I'm telling you this story is because is not good to get into big debt or to look fancy to look rich when you are not. He had a huge debt and everything was on credit. He was lying to himself and becoming a slave to the bankers. At the end of the story it was too late to help him. He lost his cars, the wife was mad because they took her BMW, he lost his boat, he lost his house and he couldn't pay the credit cards either.

If you are going to buy anything on credit, pay it off in 30 days or less unless you are paying 0% interest. If you are getting a mortgage, pay it off in 15 years or less. Don't buy a new car if you are struggling even if you qualify, even if you only put $1,000 down. If you are buying a car on credit, pay it off in less than 12 months; if you cannot do 12 months at least pay it off in 18 months. Choose to be financially independent first before you get into a big debt with a car.

If you are prepared for possible economic downturns, you will lower your risk. How can you lower your risk in this case? Try to have more savings, and don't get into too much bad debt, buy assets that will take care of your liabilities, he could have bought a house for $400,000 or less, not a million dollar home and he should have paid it off in 15 years or less.

I know that buying is an emotional thing, but think twice when you are making a big purchase or a small purchase. Don't be that guy. He was willing to give the bank over a million dollars in just interest if he decided to pay it off in 30 years, over one million dollar in interest debt in liability; his house was not an asset, it was a liability. Who knows where he is living now? Maybe he's just renting the house next door. Remember, don't buy liabilities; buy assets. I hope you can learn something from this lesson.

By the way, if you know anyone who is behind on payments or going into foreclosure, tell them to go to this website www.AlanStopsForeclosure.com so I can help them and tell them not to wait too long. Don't wait till the last moment because if they do, it is going to be too late.

CHAPTER 3

Money Management

How can anyone know where there money is going if they don't know how to manage it or control it. Having control of your money is key, especially your expenses. I have seen wealthy people ending up broke because they didn't control their expenses correctly; they buy liabilities instead of assets, and then they lose their nice cars, they lose the big boat, and the big mansion as well. How can someone set spending and saving goals if they don't know where their money is going? The answer is simple—you need to manage your money correctly whether you make twenty thousand a year or twenty million a year.

When you manage it correctly, you start to see a clear picture of how much money you have, on what you spend it on, and how much money there is to invest.

I was in a seminar and I met this guy who was making 500k a year, but he was also spending 500k a year; obviously, by the end of the year the money was gone. He never had a million dollars in his account and you probably wonder how come he never became a millionaire. The reason was simple—he didn't know how to manage his money correctly; he didn't have control of his expenses. He knew how to make money, but not how to manage it. Once he was speaking and sharing his story, I found out it was deep in his subconscious mind, his financial Thermostat, as T. Harv Eker calls it. The seed that was planted in his mind was to make that money and to spend that money as soon as he made it. There are people like that all over the world, but they start small. There are people that make $18,000 a year and spend $18,000 a year and then they program themselves to do that and they are not even aware. Years later, they make $55,000 a year and spend about $50,000 to $55,000 a year. Then they complain they can't save because of bills—the motorcycle payment, their mortgage payment, the furniture and the trip they took to Hawaii on credit too and so on.

This is what some economists calls Parkinson's law—when expenses rise to meet income over 80% of the population in America do that and then they wonder why there are so many bankruptcies in this country. My advice would be to program your mind correctly. Save to invest; don't save forever either, learning where to put your money is the key to your financial success, don't spent everything you make. Lower your expenses and create a big fat saving account, control your money have a budget whether you are making very little or a lot of money.

The upcoming example is one of the best ways to have control of your money. Figure out how are you controlling your money or where is it going; you can adjust this and make it your own. Figure out where you are right now and ask yourself where you want to be. Remember you already managing your money the question is are you doing it smart or poorly and how are you doing it, you can adjust this numbers whether you make $1,500 a month or a million a month. How much of your money is going in Education, Playing, Donating, LTS = Long Term Saving, Inv = Investments/Assets, Utilities. Most of it will go in Utilities at the beginning, the idea is to know where your money is going and adjust the numbers the way you want.

Example:

Play	10% or	15% or	25% or	10%
Education	5%	10%	1%	10%
Donate	5%	10%	1%	15%
LTS	20%	15%	1%	25%
Inv/Assets	30%	20%	2%	30%
Utilities	30%	30%	70%	10%

There is no right or wrong answer. The idea is to know where your money is going and where you want to be. If you invest in the right education you will have financial freedom. This may not happen overnight, but mean while you are saving you can get educated and figure out where to invest. Check your bank statement often and see where your money is being distributed, start there and manage your money wisely.

Get a pen and paper and look at your monthly income and figure out how much of your monthly income is going in and how is being distributed.

Utilities you can add this to bills like rent, light, water etc…

Play could be like going on vacation, buying some toys etc…

Education could be an online classes, seminar, college, a mentor, books etc…

Donate could be your favor charities or your favor church or any good deeds that is to help and benefit others.

LTS is Long Term Saving could be for Investments purpose, for education, etc…

Investments is to buy Assets or to create an asset it could be for real estate, Stocks, Forex, a franchise, businesses etc…

Savings Plan

Pay yourself first and resolve to set aside a minimum of 5% to 10% of your salary for savings BEFORE you start paying your bills; if that is too easy, then try to save more 10% to 20%. Better yet, have money automatically taken away from your paycheck and deposited into a separate account. If you cannot save 5% to 10%, try to save at least 1%. Anybody can save 1% there are no excuses. Then do 2% and then 3%, 4% until you reach your goal. I created a plan for you, whether you want to save 1% or 30% or more just figure out your number and continue to improve it. By the way, don't save forever save to invest. But before you invest, get educated the best investment you can do is in your education, the right education, and the reason I say don't save forever is because of inflation, taxes and you don't want to lose good deals either. This are some good ideas use them, borrow them and apply it into your life.

<u>Saving Plan Examples</u>:

Johnny Makes $2,000 a month = $24,000 a year

<u>Save</u>	<u>Monthly</u>	<u>Year 1</u>	<u>Year 2</u>
1%	$20	$240	$480
2%	$40	$480	$960
3%	$60	$720	$1,420
5%	$100	$1,200	$2,400
8%	$160	$1,920	$3,840
10%	$200	$2,400	$4,800

Save	Monthly	Year 1	Year 2
20%	$400	$4,800	$9,600
30%	$600	$7,200	$14,400

Maria Makes $3,500 a month = $42,000 a year

Save	Monthly	Year 1	Year 2
1%	$35	$420	$840
2%	$70	$840	$1,680
3%	$105	$1,260	$2,520
5%	$175	$2,100	$4,200
8%	$280	$3,360	$6,720
10%	$350	$4,200	$8,400
20%	$700	$8,400	$16,800
30%	$1,050	$12,600	$25,200

Eduardo Makes $6,250 a month = $75,000 a year

Save	Monthly	Year 1	Year 2
3%	$187.50	$2,250	$4,500

5%	$312.50	$3,750	$7,500
8%	$500.00	$6,000	$12,000
10%	$625.00	$7,500	$15,000
20%	$1,250.00	$15,000	$30,000
30%	$1,875.00	$22,500	$45,000
55%	$3,437.50	$41,250	$82,500

When it comes to savings, create another bank account keep yourself from spending it on liabilities. Put it there and do not touch it at all just imaging the money is not there. The main goal is to save to invest, not to save for expenses and liabilities; save and mean while LEARN about investing and then you invest, LEARN as much as you possible can, and then invest your money.

I don't believe in savings forever save for a purpose and the purpose should be to create more wealth remember there is always inflation, make smart decisions with your money liabilities are not great decisions even thou everybody have liabilities, but a lot people like to have big liabilities because they like to have big expenses and then they wonder why they can't save any money. Learn to save; be self-disciplined and while you are saving learn as much as you can even if you don't have $100 on savings, learning and applying this techniques is the key to financial freedom.

Basics of Accounting

Accounting is money coming in and money coming out. It is the process of keeping a healthy financial account and is the way of managing your money in a period of time, usually every two weeks, a month, quarter or yearly in which financial statements are prepared to reflect a company's cash flows.

Assets = An asset puts money in your pocket, and liability takes money out of it.

Examples of an Assets are:

Stocks ~ Bonds ~ Mutual Funds ~ Retirement Funds ~ Income of Real Estate you own ~ Net Value of Businesses you own ~ Debt owed to you

Gold & Silver are an asset only when you sell it, if you are not making any money with it every month is not an asset.

Liabilities = Liabilities are debts it takes money out of your pocket.

Examples of Liabilities are:

Credit Cards ~ Taxes ~ Personal loans ~ Mortgages ~ Car loans ~ Student loans

Or any other debt that is taking money out of your pocket, like membership in a gym or a websites that are charging you monthly payments.

Income

Wages or salary ~ Tips ~ Interest on Investments ~ Dividends ~ Rent from real estate ~ Businesses income ~ Royalties ~ Capital Gains.

Expenses

Taxes ~ Credit card payments ~ Home mortgage payments ~ Car loan payments ~ Utility payments ~ Grocery Bills ~ Travel ~ Entertainment ~ All other personal expenses

Net worth = Assets – Liabilities

Net Income = Gross Income – Expenses

Example:

A small apartment building with 27 units is for sale for an asking price of $3,000,000. You are able to negotiate and get it for $2,750,000 and each unit has different prices.

Units	Price Per Unit	Monthly	Annual Income
16	$850	$13,600	$163,200

2	$900	$1,800	$21,600
5	$750	$3,750	$45,000
1	$925	$925	$11,100
3	$950	$2,850	$34,200
Total Rental Income		$22,925.00	$275,100
Laundry $500/Mo		$500	$6,000
Total Annual Income			$281,100
Gross Income			$281,100

Your Total Annual Income is your Total Gross Income.

Expenses & Liabilities	
Real Estate Taxes	$23,798
Insurance	$6,684

Water and Trash	$8,328
Gas	$1,740
Electricity	$4,560
Pool Maintenance	$1,800
Other Misc. Expenses:	$5,000
Vacancy 2%(Based on rental income)	$5,628
Management	$18,000
Total Expenses:	$75,538.00

Total Gross Income	$281,100.00
Total Expenses	$75,538.00
Net Operating Income	**$205,562.00**

You add all the income and add all the expenses and subtract the Total Gross Income, minus the Total Expenses = Net Operating Income $205,562.00. This will be the result if the property was paid cash.

Let's say if you buy with a mortgage putting 20% down, the asking price is $2,750,000 the loan would be $2,200,000 with $550,000 down, your monthly payment would be around $11,147.08 this would include principle and interest, and yearly mortgage expenses would be $133,764.96, you add the yearly mortgage expenses with the rest of the expenses that are $75,538.00 you will have a total expenses of $209,302.96.

Now you know your total Gross Income and your Total Expenses, subtract that and you get the Net Operating Income.

Gross Income: $281,100.00

Total Expenses: $209,302.96

Net Operating Income = $71,797.04. This would be your yearly profit with a mortgage. In this case your mortgage is a good debt because it brings you money every month and every year.

In a lot of cases, you can put less money down or NO money at all if you use creative finance techniques, like using private lending, seller finance, Master Lease Option, equity of the property, Join venture partner, personal loan, credit cards, mortgage, etc…. If you want to invest in real estate and do big deals you can go to www.investingWithAlan.com and start investing with Alan.

This is just an example of a 27-unit apartment, if you do a 1,000 unit the number is going to be bigger, if you do a duplex the number is going to be smaller, if you do a shopping center it will be a different financial statement than a Gas Station and a Gas Station financial statement would be different than a Senior Facility or any other business. If you know how to read your numbers, the number itself would tell you a story and this is important if you want to start a business

Successful stock investors that have become millionaires and even billionaires understand this and they go over the financial statement of the company before buying shares of that stocks and because they know the numbers and where the market is going they are able to invest with confidence.

I have talk to a few accountants over the years and is funny because a few of them have told me the same thing, most business owners that have a business don't have a plan, and I ask myself if they are going to have a business they should start with a good foundation, you must have a plan a good vision statement of where you want the company to go, the same accountant have told me that most business owners don't know how to manage their finance instead the money is managing them and then they get frustrated, and some businesses they don't even advertise that's why they don't have any sales, and if they do advertise they spend too much money in marketing that don't work and they don't even know if they are having ROI, return on investing, they don't know how to track their advertising money.

If you are going to advertise online, you can successfully track your advertising money but if you do off line marketing it may be difficult to do unless you have created a good system to track your advertising money.

You can buy a few personal financial statements sheets in Office Depot for less than $10 or you can probably download it in the internet for free. Just Google Free Personal Financial Statements sheets if you are in business there are a lot of good software you can use and there are also apps that you can have in your phone.

Mortgage Payment and Paying It Off In Less Than 15 Years.

This is just an example of a $100,000 Mortgage. This doesn't include your taxes, insurance or your down payment (Some People pay 3.5% Down with FHA, others pay conventional 10% or 20% down; this is just a good example of a $100,000 Mortgage only)

$100,000 Mortgage Repayment Summary

Mortgage Monthly Payment only	$506.69

Total of 360 Payments	$182,406.71
Total Interest Paid in 30 years	$82,406.71
Started date	Jan 2016
Pay-off Date	Jan 2046

2016	Payment	Principal	Interest	Total Interest	Balance
Jan	$506.69	$131.69	$375.00	$375.00	$99,868.31
Feb	$506.69	$132.18	$374.51	$749.51	$99,736.14
Mar	$506.69	$132.67	$374.01	$1,123.52	$99,603.46
Apr	$506.69	$133.17	$373.51	$1,497.03	$99,470.29
May	$506.69	$133.67	$373.01	$1,870.04	$99,336.62
Jun	$506.69	$134.17	$372.51	$2,242.56	$99,202.44
Jul	$506.69	$134.68	$372.01	$2,614.56	$99,067.77
Aug	$506.69	$135.18	$371.50	$2,986.07	$98,932.59
Sep	$506.69	$135.69	$371.00	$3,357.07	$98,796.90
Oct	$506.69	$136.20	$370.49	$3,727.55	$98,660.70
Nov	$506.69	$136.71	$369.98	$4,097.53	$98,523.99

2016	Payment	Principal	Interest	Total Interest	Balance
Dec	$506.69	$137.22	$369.46	$4,467.00	$98,386.77

If you add all the interest from January 2016 to December 2016, you will get a total of $4,466.99 in Interest only. Do you see how much money you are giving away to the bank in one year alone? And you have 29 years left to go. That's the reason you want to pay more in principal, and some people will continue to have debt even after 30 years. In one year, you pay about $1,619.27 in principal it when from $100,000 loan to $98,386.77

If you only pay **$50 extra** for principal every month and you do that for **10 years,** you be **saving between 3 & 4 years of mortgage payments**. And that is only with $50 imagine if you are paying at least $300 to $500 in principal every month.

When you make your payment, send an extra check for principal only, send a check for 3 months in advance if you can pay for Feb, March, April as principal and the next month for 3 more months of principal only, if you do that you will pay off your house in about 10 to 12 years, instead of 30 or 40 years. And you definitely want to save money because the bank is charging you high interest by month, NOT by the year and is all compound interest.

Pay principal for three months in advance, You will be able to pay a full year payment in 4 months, and you will be able to pay a 10 year payment in about four years, saving you six long years of headache. If you continue, you will pay a 20 year payment in about 8 years and a 30 year payment between 10 to 12 years, saving you about 18 to 20 years of headache and a lot of money.

Principal (when you pay in Jan you pay principal for 3 months, when you pay in February you pay principal for 3 more months, when you pay for March you pay principal for 3 more months.) You just did a one year payment in 4 months.

Jan payment + 3 months in principal   Feb/ Mar/ Apr

Feb Payment + 3 months in principal   May/ Jun/ Jul

Mar Payment + 3 months in principal Aug/ Sep/ Oct

Apr Payment + 3 months in principal Nov/ Dec/ Jan

If you cannot do that do 1 or 2 months in principal, but always pay principal, or at least $50 but always pay principal.

$400,000 Mortgage Repayment Summary

Mortgage Monthly Payment only	$2,026.74

Total of 360 Payments	$729,626.85
Total Interest Paid	$329,626.85
Started Date	Jan, 2016
Pay-off Date	Jan, 2046

2016	Payment	Principal	Interest	Total Interest	Balance
Jan	$2,026.74	$526.74	$1,500.00	$1,500.00	$399,473.26
Feb	$2,026.74	$528.72	$1,498.02	$2,998.02	$398,944.54
Mar	$2,026.74	$530.70	$1,496.04	$4,494.07	$398,413.84
Apr	$2,026.74	$532.69	$1,494.05	$5,988.12	$397,881.15
May	$2,026.74	$534.69	$1,492.05	$7,480.17	$397,346.47
Jun	$2,026.74	$536.69	$1,490.05	$8,970.22	$396,809.77
Jul	$2,026.74	$538.70	$1,488.04	$10,458.26	$396,271.07
Aug	$2,026.74	$540.72	$1,486.02	$11,944.28	$395,730.35
Sept	$2,026.74	$542.75	$1,483.99	$13,428.26	$395,187.59
Oct	$2,026.74	$544.79	$1,481.95	$14,910.22	$394,642.81
Nov	$2,026.74	$546.83	$1,479.91	$16,390.13	$394,095.97

2016	Payment	Principal	Interest	Total Interest	Balance
Dec	$2,026.74	$548.88	$1,477.86	$17,867.99	$393,547.09

If you add all the interest from January 2016 to December 2016, you will get a total of $17,867.98 in Interest only. Do you see how much money you are giving away to the bank in one year alone and you have 29 years left to go, that's why you want to pay more in principal, you don't want to be in debt for 30 or 40 years and throwing your money away for no reason. In one year you pay about $6,452.91 in principal, but in interest debt you pay about three times more, it when from $400,000 loan to $393,547.09 pay more in principal than what you do in interest if you do that you will pay your house in eight to 15 years.

Most people will pay about the same amount of what they have borrow in interest and sometimes even more because of the interest rate, refinance and because a lot of people have the habit of paying the minimum payment only.

Remember this doesn't include Taxes, Insurance and probably PMI, Private Mortgage Insurance, it all depends on how much down you put, in the state that you are buying, Florida is different than California, Texas is different than New York, any other state are different, it all depends where are you buying, how much PMI you are paying 1% or half it all depends, Wells Fargo mortgage and interest is different than a mortgage broker interest and loan, instead go and find out with your mortgage broker, or go to Google and put mortgage calculator there are many free websites and software you can use. Your goal should be to pay it off in less than 15 years the sooner the better.

The average person will pay off his house in 35 to 50 years for three reasons.

1- The average person will pay $0.00 extra in principal every month; please don't do that ever, even if you don't have much pay at least $50 the more the better. There are good financial softwares that can help you figure out what you need to do to pay it off in 7 to 15 years.

2- The average person will refinance between 2 to 5 times in about 40 years, getting into more debt, if you are getting money out make sure you do it to buy an asset like real estate and make sure there is enough equity in the property, if you are not 100% sure of what you are doing don't do it.

3- There may be about two or three economy crashes in about 30 years and if you are not ready, this may hurt you, in every economy crash, there will be more unemployment & foreclosures make sure this doesn't happen to you.

What do you think is better—paying your house off in 10 years or 40 years? I think you know the answer. My two brothers will pay off their house in four or five years and the reason they do that is because they are not average; they understand their numbers. Please understand your numbers. It can save you years of hard work and stress. You don't have to pay it off in five years, but 15 years is great and that's something most people can do.

CHAPTER 4

THE SMART WAY TO PAY OFF ALL HIGH INTEREST DEBT

The best way to handle debt is to stay out of it in the first place, unless it's good debt. Mismanaging your debt through overspending or getting into high interest rates can quickly hurt you in the long run. Remember to stay away from "buy now, buy now pay later" sales; they are all over the place on TV, Radio, magazines, in a lot of shopping centers and malls that you go to. They are good marketers; they will tell you 0% Interest for 15 months buy now, buy now and then after 15 months, they add up the entire debt into a 18% interest on average. Don't get me wrong—if you can pay it off in less than 15 months and is something you really need, go for it. But it takes self-discipline to do that. Take a look at your finances and income and always ask if that's a priority. Is that an asset or a liability? It is okay to have a consumer mentality, but is much greater and better to have an investor mentality. There is a difference between need and want; be aware of that. Be careful with those buying emotions those buying decisions. Don't get into high interest loans, don't get into debt just because you want to pay yourself first; pay yourself with debit not credit.

Some loans are good especially for education, your first home, more real estate, a good business, some good assets that will pay for themselves. But make sure you have a plan or a good business plan and a good vision of the business plan.

Real Estate is a good investments, it could be a good asset but at the same time it could be a bad investment if you don't know what you are doing, same as stocks it could be a great asset but if you don't know what you are doing it could be a liability. Borrowing money to start a business is a good idea but if you don't have a plan, a good vision and if you are not prepared to start a business maybe you should think twice, create a plan be prepared mentally, emotionally, spiritually, have some knowledge about your business, have a plan, have some strategies and then put that plan into action.

What are Warren Buffet's rules when it comes to money? Rule number 1 is don't ever lose money. Rule Number 2 is don't ever forget rule number 1. Credit card debt of $10,000 at 18% interest or more could be worth more than $20,000 with compound interest in the long run, if you pay the minimum. What do you think it could happen in four years? You will be wondering why the debt didn't get any lower.

Why do you think the banks and the financial Institutions make billions of dollars? They make billions because of interest rates, your credit cards, your car loan and your mortgage. They make millions daily just with the late fees. The system they have created is for their own benefit, not for yours. The system is to get you into debt and to take your money. You work hard just to make them wealthy. It is time for us to stop that. It is all about habits; create a good financial habit not a bad financial habit.

The difference between the rich and the poor is that the rich know how to manage their money well; they created a good financial habits and they don't fall into that trap of the consumer mentality. As a general rule, do not finance anything for too long, even if they tell you that you are approve, unless is a good debt be smart about it and always check for the numbers interest rate and the years of the loans. Home loans, real estate loans, and business loans are okay to go out for longer, but still look at the numbers and always send an extra check every month for the principle; keep track of your finances.

A friend of mine bought a new car when she told me the numbers how much was the car and the interest and the period of the loan, I realize that she was giving them about $22,000 in just interest and that's for a car and she only makes $9 an hour, you do not want to do that, you don't need to through your money that way. What is she going to have when she finishes paying off that debt? She is going to have a very old car. Even the guys that work in the car dealership fall for that trap, I remember the time when I went to a car dealership just to drive a few cars, the guy who was trying to sell me a car told me his story. He bought a new car for

$55,000 and put 10% down just to get approved. This is the guy who makes about $22,000 a year that lives in an apartment with his wife and kids. I don't know about you, but I think that's a really bad financial decision.

Don't get into debt you don't need.

Avoid getting into those high expenses and liabilities that all they do is to take your money every single month, don't get into more liabilities don't get so emotional when you see a shining object just don't buy everything you see and if you are going to buy, buy cash or debit not on credit, if you are getting something that says 0% interest for 12 months or 18 month pay it off before they start charging you high interest. Think prosperity and abundance.

Transferring Your Credit Card Balance.

If you are paying credit cards debt at a high interest rate, look for the card that has the highest interest rate, then get another credit card with 0% interest for 18 months and transfer that to the new card; at least you will have 0% interest for 18 months. Once you do that, your goal should be to pay that card in less than 18 months, or just transfer it to a credit card that you already have that is low interest. Example if you have a credit card debt that is 24% and another credit card that is 12% you may want to transfer the debt of the credit card that have 24% to the one that have 12% they may let you do that call your credit card company, talk to them.

Look at your finance and set that goal and achieve that goal. Pay off the credit card with the highest interest first and then continue with the second credit card with the highest interest and then continue with the third credit card with the highest interest rate, but also take in consideration the amount that you have borrow and see which one would be better for you to pay off first.

Avoid Parkinson's Law.

This is when your expenses are the same as your income or your expenses are greater than your income. People who become wealthy or financially independent do not fall into this trap. But most of the middle class falls into this trap because they spend everything they make in credit; they say they are going to pay it off later but never do.

Henry Ford a very successful business man with a successful company. A lot of people who had study the biography and life of Henry Ford they have says that he did very well in his business and he became one of the richest man in the world in his time. But in his business there was a time that he was losing up to a million dollar a day, imaging losing a million dollar a day every single day even thou he was making thousands of cars daily there was a time he was losing a million dollars daily, he could have easily lost everything that he had built but he didn't he had a lot of money in reserve to back him up and he still came up on top. Now why do I tell you this story? Because if Henry Ford didn't have that money in reserve, he could have easily lost it all. So whether you make $20,000 or millions of dollars every year, don't let your expenses rises to increase your income, a lot of people that win the lotto do that all the time, a lot of people create a bad habit that if they make more they will spend more. Whether you are poor, middle class, or rich, be careful because expenses could rise to meet income, don't get into high interest debt, but instead pay off your debt pay your bills on time, start with the debt that have the highest interest or big amount do your math grab a financial calculator or software, make sure that there is enough money going into principle, if you do that you are going to avoid on getting into the trap of Parkinson law.

The decisions you make about borrowing, spending, and paying bills when you're 24 can still haunt you when you're 34 or even 44. Keep your credit card debt as low as possible. Focus on raising your credit score by paying on time, and thinking carefully before opening any new accounts. If you are going to use credit, use it for gas, groceries, and then pay it off in less than 30 days.

If you are going to use credit use it to buy good debt not bad debt. If you are using it and paying it all off that's good.

Be Your Own Debt Settlement.

You can use a debt settlement company; there is nothing wrong with that. But if you use them, they may charge you an upfront fee, a small down payment, and they may charge you between 15% to 25% of what they have settle.

The best option will be to do it yourself instead of having a company doing it for you, once the bad debt is in the three credit bureaus—Transunion, Equifax, and Experian—you will be able to negotiate and lower your debt, you can call the company that is handling your debt and offer between 45% to 75% off, they can deal with you directly without any problem. This is something you can do on your own by calling the companies that have your debt or send them a letter they are willing to work with you. Know your number and give them your number, you should start by getting a 75% off if they say no tell them to work with you and call them back in 2 or 3 weeks and offer 70% off, don't tell them you want 70% off you must know your number already.

Example:

Debt is $20,000 you offer 75% off that will be $15,000 discount, you will offer $5,000

Debt is $20,000 you offer 70% off that will be $14,000 discount, you will offer $6,000

Debt is $20,000 you offer 65% off that will be $13,000 discount, you will offer $7,000

The best way to avoid a debt is to stay out of it in the first place. If you do a debt settlement, it is going to hurt your credit score for a few months even a few years, until you pay the debt. Once you pay the debt, tell them to take it out of the three credit bureaus, ask them even while you are paying off the debt they may do it if not wait until your debt is paid off and then ask them to take it out. If you pay for the debt cash, they will take it out ASAP from the bureaus.

Get educated.

There are videos, books, DVDs, in the library that you can get for free for a few days or weeks there are a lot of great ideas out there, by the way the same info you can find it in the internet and there are software that can help you pay off your debt faster, you may have to pay for the software it may be worthy.

Don't cut your credit cards.

I heard a lot of people giving advice to other people that they should cut their credit cards, I wouldn't do that because it will hurt your credit score, instead learn how to make money with your credit cards, it may take some time for you to learn it may take some discipline, but don't cut your credit card is not a good idea, if you have to because you are always buying liabilities with it, then you choose if you want to do that or not I will not do it but is your choice.

Always pay more for principle.

Pay principles for credit cards, for your car, your mortgage, for student loan, personal loan etc… One good thing you can do is to use Auto Pay if you are able to do that do it. Don't ever pay the minimum. If a credit card debt is $2,000 and minimum is $45, pay it off in 10 payments of $200 or four payments of $500 or two payments of $1,000, especially if the credit card has high interest. Do your numbers make the best decision for that moment and for the long run. Another good example is the one I used for the mortgage payment and paying it off in 15 years or less.

20% to 40% of your wealth could be spend in interest only in your lifetime. Get in the habit of paying for principle and learn more about money.

CHAPTER 5

WEALTH CREATION

There is an old saying: where energy flows attention goes. When you focus on problems, you'll have more problems; when you focus on possibilities and success you will have more opportunities and success. Getting out of debt is good, but what could be better is to focus on wealth creation, to create wealth.

Just focus on wealth creation, **Focus On Abundance.** When you focus on abundance and wealth creation and how to create wealth, the universe or God will send you opportunities of wealth. But you have to be aware so you can take action. Commit yourself to excellence, choose to be the best, work fast, save your capital, and the more you save the more you will have and the more it will grow, think success and expect success all the time, learn about investments, believe you are going to be the best at it and you will see how God and the universe will help you and it will open doors, believe that wealth is coming to you, but remember you have to help yourselves, everything is cause and effect if you don't do nothing, nothing is going to happens your finances will not change, but if you do something about it and you choose to move towards your goal soon you will see that your goal is moving towards you and that's what you want.

Learn as much as you can to become financially independent and don't trust stock brokers or real estate agents when it comes to your investments. Most of them they don't know much about wealth creation that's why they work for that company instead of working for themselves or doing investments on their own.

Don't get me wrong; you can still learn a lot when you are a newbie they can guide you to get Mutual Funds, Index funds, Your IRA & 401k, but most of them don't know how to trade stocks, options or forex successfully, but is ok go talk to a few of them get some experience, I will talk about this investments later on in other chapters. Let's talk about creating wealth, later on in this book am going to give you even more tips, but for now let's start with this.

The law of abundance.

People who succeed focus on success that's the reason they are successful, people that started with nothing and became rich is because they believe that it was possible for them, at the beginning it starts small they start thinking well maybe I can do it let me save to invest mean while am saving am going to be learning, they start saving 200 a month every month. They created the habit and then they see more money and then they save more, and now they have more savings, then they save even more now is 300 a month and then it becomes 400 a month and the law of abundance is working for them and they don't even understand how but is working and then it becomes $600 a month, $750 a month, $1,000 a month, $2,000 a month and while they are being saving they have also being learning they started with one book and now they read over 40 books, is like compound interest or just like the snowball effect, the same goes with everything. For a business owner at the beginning it could be hard to open a business is just him and one employee and then it becomes 3 employees and then 10, 15, 25, 45, 65 employees and 6 years later he could end up having over 500 employees. Always think abundance always think big, think success. Donald Trump says if you are going to be thinking anything you might as well think big, thinking big is abundance, thinking prosperity is abundance, thinking success and greatness is abundance, thinking and focusing in doubling and tripling your income and doing something about it is abundance, think abundance think about what you want, you cannot create abundance if you don't believe in abundance, and the law of abundance goes together with faith, you have to believe in abundance so it can work, the more abundance you have the more you are going to believe in yourself and the more you believe the more abundance you will have. There is an old saying that says that the first million is the hardest and is true, after your first million the second million is a little bit easier and then the third million, and then the fifth and then ten millions and then it gets a lot easier, think prosperity believe in abundance. But the problem is that most people don't think abundance they just want to get a job and once they get a job they stay there for years and they don't even try to grow and if they grow they grow a little bit why because of their way of thinking. Let me tell you that the things stopping people from succeeding is their own beliefs.

Powerful Leverage

OPM = Other People Money

OPT = Other People Time

OPI = Other People Ideas

OPE = Other People Everything.

When it comes to using powerful leverage you always want to create a win-win for everyone, if you cannot create a win-win for everyone don't do it at all. Take your time in learning this powerful leverage techniques first & be committed to your word when using this techniques, the most successful companies in the world use powerful leverage and they do it all the time. Remember WIN-WIN for everyone for you and your employees, for you and the bank that is going to lend you the money, for you and your business partners, your equity partner, or any other member in your team. Let's start with some examples.

Good Debt.

We spoke about bad debt before; the idea is to get out of bad debt fast, now we are going to talk about the fun part good debt. Good debt is OPM other people's money, imaging borrowing money at 6% and you used that money and you invested in something that can make you 14% how much money would you borrow? I would borrow as much as I possibly can if I can borrow 10 billion dollars at 6% and put it on something that makes 14%. Why not? I believe anybody will accept that I know I will. Ok let's be more realistic.

As an example let's say we only borrow a million dollar putting the asset the property as collateral, I would look around search for good properties with good cap rate, in a good neighborhood and I find a 20 unit apartment for $1,000,000 or less we can buy the property all cash or getting a finance by the owner or the bank, we do a master lease option with the owner, the main goal is to put very little money down if I do it through the bank it may ask me between 20% to 40% down and that is a lot, I would rather put 10% to 15% down or less, so I probably negotiate something with the owner to create a win-win situation for him and for myself. He could probably finance 80% of the property and then I borrow the 20% from other sources like a personal loan or credit card or another investor at a low interest, and I probably didn't have to use the $1,000,000 I borrowed in the first place. And the property is making cash flow a good residual income at a good rate and the property is getting pay by itself.

A lady I met at an event was talking about gold, silver, and jewelry. I asked her how she started her jewelry business and she told me that she started with a credit card of $300 dollars about 6 years ago. She bought a piece of jewelry and sold it online and made a little bit of money and she did it again and again. Every time she had profit, she paid her credit card and reinvested the rest soon she was using three and four credit cards every time. She was using her credit card to buy jewelry and to sell that jewelry online; the banks that lent her the money on credit gave her even more money. She was using credit cards to make money and she told me that she was always paying on time and that she received letters in the mail saying that she qualified for a credit card up to $50,000. She was able to quit her job, work from home and be able to expand time with her two children, she was able to make up to $55,000 a year in profit using other people money—credit cards.

I have worked with several investors who use credit cards to buy real estate, residential and commercial. They have 20 to 40 credit cards with a limit of $20,000 to $50,000 and they were able to become rich doing that. They also used personal loans, business loans, private money or hard money to flip real estate or to buy commercial real estate with a good cap rate, they buy assets and they make sure the assets take care of all the liabilities. Let's say that the limit on a credit card of capital one is $25,000. They will call capital one and ask them to send him a check of $25,000 they will grab that money and put it as a down payment, they make sure that the property they just bought makes enough money to pay for the mortgage, taxes, insurance and any other expenses that they may have including the money they just borrow, They used credit cards to buy an asset that produces residual income, cash flow and they do that all the time with more than 20 credit cards, they used good debt to created wealth.

I also know this investor from Texas that he did the same thing but with 9 credit cards and a small personal loan that his brother got from the bank to buy a 44 unit apartment, the reason they can do this is because they understand the numbers, they understand the debt, the risk and the ROI which it means return on investment, they bought a 44 unit apartment without using any of their own money. As you can see good debt is powerful leverage.

Christopher Columbus: A Nothing-Down Deal.

Let's talk a little bit about history. Everybody has heard the story about Christopher Columbus but nobody have ever seen this side of the story that makes this the entire accomplishment of Christopher Columbus a reality. I am sure you have heard about the story but you probably haven't apply it in your business.

When it comes to business many people say, you need money to make money, yes is true but it doesn't have to be your money necessarily. What Christopher Columbus did is a good example that you can apply in your business whether you want to buy a house or you want to start a business. Christopher Columbus borrowed the money; he didn't have any money he was broke he even borrowed the three boats and discovered land but before he made his believe, dream and vision a reality he was judge, a lot of people thought he was crazy because a lot of people in those days thought the world was flat. Everybody thought that if you go through the ocean you were not going to go nowhere, he was criticized by people all the time a lot of people thought he was crazy everybody were saying the world is flat, but Christopher Columbus didn't believe that. He believe in his dream so much that he decided to borrow the money to go on a quest, even though people were criticizing him telling him that he was crazy to go through the ocean to find land even though everybody doubt him.

Queen Isabella believed in him and she decided to give him the money and three boats for him to go on that quest. The point of the story is that Christopher Columbus didn't have any money at all because he was broke. All he had was a dream a good vision and a plan he was able to share his story even though people thought he was crazy, but he believed in himself and believe in his vision. Maybe you could borrow money to start a business. Maybe you could borrow money to buy an apartment building; maybe you could borrow the money to make your vision a reality. Go create a plan and accomplish it, go and accomplish your goals and everything that you want to accomplish you could do the same thing. You can create a good win-win situation for everybody go through this journey put in your life to have the results that you want, I hope this ideas and this story can help you through your journey for success.

How Bill Gates Made his Fortune.

Bill Gates, a visionary with determination and passion, became the richest entrepreneur in the world. He is someone with a big dream but that wasn't enough to make the fortune that he made. He was into computers and development of software, he made his fortune by buying a program a software that he needed he bought it for $50,000. He used OPE Other People Everything, It was somebody else product, somebody else idea, someone else hard work and development of that product, Bill Gates just came and said you know what I need that software, I want that program this is what I need to develop what I want to develop. Bill Gates saw that opportunity. He was able to buy the software for $50,000. The company that sold the program to Bill Gates they shouldn't have never sold it to him the software, they should have licenses to him but they didn't do that, Bill Gate saw a great opportunity and he took action fast he went and bought it, and then he took that program to IBM and he licenses to the company to create a win-win situation, that was the key, that was what he needed to become the richest man in the world the main point of this is that he saw somebody else's product somebody else's developing somebody else's hard work it was something that he needed he came up and bought it for $50,000 and then he went and license the product to make his entire fortune. Something that it was for $50,000 made Bill gates over 50 billion dollars the main point is that you can use somebody else's ideas somebody else's product or probably partner with somebody that have what you need you could use somebody else expertise, remember he bought someone else product for very cheap for something that can make him billions of dollars you could use this idea this example in your life to go and find what you need if you cannot buy it at least partner with that person or borrow the money to buy it, if you partner with that person or that company you are create a win-win situation everybody wins, you win by using someone else product to make money, the owner of the product or the company wins because he is also making money for lending you the product or sell his product. If you don't know how to do that, I have a FREE TRAINING AS YOUR BONUS, I created 3 FREE videos that teach people how to use someone else product or software to make 40% to 90% commission or profit and you can do this using your computer and you can do it from home, you can sell training or software of other company like Yoga, Diet, Nutrition, Health and Beauty, Real Estate programs, Investments programs, or Business programs like marketing, finance etc… there are thousands if not millions of companies or people that will let you market their product and they are willing to pay you between 40% to

90% let me give you an example if you only make a million dollar of sale in one year and you make 90% commission you just put in your pocket $900,000 in 1 year and like I said there are thousands of companies like that if not millions just go to my website to get your FREE Bonus, your FREE Training videos at www.TheOnlineBusiness.Info and the best thing is that you can do this from home and you don't have to talk to nobody unless you want to but you don't have to.

Go to www.TheOnlineBusiness.Info to watch the three FREE Videos I created, once you are in the website just put your name and email and I will send you the FREE Training videos to your email get the training get the education and start making money from home, the best part of this is that you don't have to buy the products to do this business am going to show you how to do it so you can become your own boss and be able to work from home.

Mark Zuckerberg

Everything starts with an idea, the creation of Facebook started with an idea an stolen idea but it was an idea, the founder and creator of Facebook Mark Zuckerberg a college dropout. How did he came up with this idea? He stole or borrowed the idea from other people.

Many of you already know the story. There were two brothers and his business partner and they were developing a website but they couldn't succeed the way they wanted to.

One day they found a guy who knew how to develop websites and programs who was really good at it, this person was Mark Zuckerberg. They told him their plans, the ideas, the vision; they wanted to create a social website for the Harvard students so they can talk with each other and put comments on each other profile. Something similar to Facebook but they didn't know how to develop that program. That's when Mark Zuckerberg borrowed that idea.

The two brothers and his partner they should have had a contract with Mark Zuckerberg so it could be impossible for him to still his idea but they didn't.

Mark Zuckerberg used OPI, other people ideas, to create Facebook. Then he used OPM to grow it, from Harvard, to all universities, to worldwide. The main point of this is that you can use other people's ideas, other people knowledge. The same way am giving you some good ideas and some good tips you can use these ideas and go create your wealth borrow this ideas be creative and make it happen, one idea from this book could be worth millions of dollars or a lot more, one single idea could change your life, you can create something big, you can create a huge impact for you and your family and for thousands of people if not millions, that's what I believe that's why is very important to go to seminars listen to speakers, listen to preachers, listen to other people go to the event, read the books, listen to audio books. Go and search for the knowledge and wisdom, get more ideas all you need is one good idea to set you free financially or spiritually, one idea to get you out of the rat race one idea can make you a millionaire or a billionaire just like it did with Mark Zuckerberg and many other rich folks, go explore; go look for the right knowledge.

Jim Rohn once said that success is doing ordinary things extraordinarily well. Why not grab this belief and apply it in your life, grab an ordinary idea and make it extraordinarily well that's the same thing many successful businesses do they look at their competitors and try to make it better, they are always asking themselves what are they doing, how can we make it better than them, they are in competition with each other trying to be better than each other. Just look for the right idea and knowledge and go create something good with it, make it extraordinarily well. Make it better in quality and price, in production, better ways to develop the product or make better product than the competitors, better ways to market, better customer service etc.

Don't be like the CEO of Blockbuster. He didn't see it coming even when his wife was buying Netflix, Red box, and online Movies; that's the reason Blockbuster went out of business. He didn't improve his ideas; he didn't give the customer what they wanted but there competitors did.

Mentors, Role Models or coaches

We all have role models: parents could be our role models, people in TV could be our role model, actors, singers could be our role models. I did have plenty of role models who made a big difference in my life; one of them was my oldest brother Gianni. When I was a kid 11 - 12 year old he was in the business of Import & Export car for a few years and then he started another business, he had plenty of businesses one of the business that he have that I like is Trouble his clothing line he have about 3 or 4 stores with my other brother Carlitos Trouble is a Brand that represents the best Skate-Outlet in Peru. He also had a night club a pet shop and many more businesses what I like about my brother is that he execute what he knows he makes things happens he have being in business since he was young, probably 16-17 year old. He was always looking to buy and sell something and make a profit. Am glad I have good brothers a good sister and a good mother, My mom was a school teacher but she acts like an accounting sometimes she knows my expenses more than I do and she knows how to keep track on things, my dad is a psychologist. I wish I could say that my dad thought me a lot but he didn't, my mom was a father and a mother to me.

I Try to learn from the best and hang around with the best, Jim Rohn says it best: "your income will be the same proportion of the top 5 people you hang around with the most." Beware who you hang around with and who you listen to as well that's the reason I listen to my mentors, be careful what you listen and what you watch as well because a lot of what we listen and watch in TV is the language of the poor and middle class is not the language of wealth creation even our school teachers have that language, it is a different language a lot of people don't realize but it is even my mother have that language and she doesn't know she have it and my father as well. There is a language for everything: there is the language of the attorneys, The language of people that are in the financial world, The language of politics, the language of doctors, the language of people that lives in the ghetto, the language of gangsters and criminals, the language of successful public speakers and bad public speakers, the language of homeless people, the language of success and greatness, the language of love, we have the spiritual language, we have body language. Rap music is different than Salsa and Merengue; Heavy Metal is different than country music, the language of a six year old is different than the language of a sixty year old and we also have the language of wealth that creates wealth and is not only the language but the habit as well, 90% of the wealthy and rich have a library in their home and more than 50% of the books they have is about wealth creation or anything related to that topic.

All of my mentors that I have mentioned all of them make over $6 million a year and they all have a different language and a different habit than the person that makes $50,000 a year. If you want to create more wealth, choose your language and choose your habit and let me tell you that if you don't change nothing would change in your life. Success is something you can develop, it don't matter where you are or what situation have happen to you in the past success is something you can develop beyond where you currently are. Am not saying that one language or habit is better than the other, is just philosophy all am saying is be aware of what you want and if you have to make some changes go for it, even if it takes you a few months or years it may be worthy at the end. One of the best ways to do that is to have mentors, reading books, listen to speakers, listening to audio books, be aware of what you want and go for it. Family could be a good role model but is not enough find and search for people that are very successful and do what they do, use OPE other people everything, knowledge, ideas etc.

Prioritize Your Goals

What are your financial goals?

_____

_____

_____

Do you want to be poor, middle class, or rich? And why?

_____

_____

_____

Do you want to work for money or do you want money to work for you? And what's your plan?

_____

_____

_____

Do you want to be A) Employee / Self-employed Or

Do you want to be B) Investor & Business Person.

_____

_____

_____

Do you want to have a master mind group of leaders, Managers, Supervisor, JV partners, that can help you to create wealth for you and the company or you just want a job? Are you willing to do what it takes and learn?

_____

_____

Are you willing to save to invest?

_____

Are you willing to learn as much as you possible can about financially literacy?

_____

_____

Are you willing to do what it takes to become financially independent?

_____

_____

Do you think you can use other people's money, other people's time, and other people's ideas to get ahead financially?

_____

_____

If you had all the knowledge you need to succeed, but no money would you be able to succeed?

_____

_____

These are just a few questions, the main point of the exercise is to show you that you have choices, more than you may have ever imagined and that you need to make decisions about those choices. Too many people go from job to job or business to business without getting where they want to be financially, and one of the reasons is that they don't have a clear goal of where they want to be, create a goal make a plan to achieve it and work on that plan every single day, the main goal is to learn as much as you can and then to apply that knowledge to make it happen, decide to do it and just do it.

Decide what you want, be aware of the way you think, most people don't become wealthy or rich for two reasons.

1- They don't have the knowledge

2- They don't believe they can do it

Just like I spoke in the first chapter of Knowledge and Faith. Know how to manage your money correctly and know where to invest your money correctly so it can grow, go and search for the knowledge and once you have the knowledge believe you can do it and just do it.

If you don't believe that you can become wealthy or rich, nothing will happen; there is no hope at all.

Believe in your dreams and goals do whatever it takes to make it happens, that's the difference between people that succeed and people that don't.

Do yourself a favor—learn about money. If anything you can go to my website to learn how to make money from home so you can start a successful home based business go to www.TheOnlineBusiness.Info

If you want to be good at goal setting, and to become a master at it so you can achieve financial goals, family goals, health goals, relationship goals, get my small booklet on goal setting. It is a small booklet you can read it in a day and the content is really good and straight to the point. If you already have it congratulations, go over it a few times until you get good at it and create the habit, you can get it in www.AlanKeysToSuccess.com or just put my name Alan Eduardo in iTunes, Amazon, or Kindle.

A good goal should be to talk to a few financial planners I know it may seem that am contradicting myself because I say not to trust all of them and that they are not real investors, But they can help you get started, they can help you with a financial plan, find out how many years of experience do they have make sure they have at least seven years of experience and if you are going to invest in some index funds, mutual funds, or long term stocks ask them if they are investing their own money there if they are not ask them why.

You may not become rich with the advice of financial planners, but at least you can be secured and stable. If you want to be wealthy or rich continue with your education and create another type of financial plan.

The Rule of 72

The Rule of 72 is a rule financial experts use, successful investors use it, experts in the economy use it. The rule of 72 is used to find out how long it will take for an investment to double.

Just take the number 72 and divide it by the interest rate you want to earn. That number gives you the approximate number of years it will take for your investment to double.

$72 \div 10\% = 7.2$ years. In this case it will take 7 years and 2 months for your money to double, whether you invest $5,000 or millions of dollars the rule still the same.

Let's say you only invest $10,000 and you don't add any more money, how long it will take for your money do double at 6% and 12% .

Years	6%	12%
0	$10,000	$10,000
6		$20,000
12	$20,000	$40,000
18		$80,000

24	$40,000	$160,000
30		$320,000
36	$80,000	$640,000
42		$1,280,000
48	$160,000	$2,560,000

$72 \div 12\% = 6$ years for your money to double, that means that your money will double every 6 years.

$72 \div 6\% = 12$ years for your money to double, that's the reason I put 12 years, 24, 36 & 48 years because every 12 years your money will double, according to the rule of 72.

Some successful financial experts who work in the banks understand this rule, some financial advisors understand this rule. Some smart people in the economy understand this rule and smart investors like myself understand this rule, and this is just an example without adding a single dollar every month, just imaging if you are adding $30 or $50 extra every month, your money will add up huge with compound interest. The more money you add every month, the bigger the amount of the return. Let's say you add between $100 to $300 every month at 6% only your money would have become millions of dollars a lot faster.

Monopoly

Money is what you want it to be. It can be a blessing it can be a curse, it could be freedom or it can make you its slave. It can be an asset it or a liability, it could be like a game if you choose too what makes money risky is the person is not the money or the investment. I am sure you remember the game Monopoly is a fun game but when it comes to real life is not that fun for some people for some it is. I remember when the bank will lend the players money to buy the green house and if you have plenty of green houses, you can trade it for a red hotel. It will be great to get the red hotel with a restaurant in it, I haven't done that yet but I know I will. When it comes to this game and life you have the dice in your hands every single day, every month and every year through the dice and move ahead in life, my two brothers and I are playing this game but only with the green houses, soon will be the red hotel or the apartment buildings, sometimes in real life it takes time to make the next move, but when it comes our turn we make a move and it doesn't have to be real estate either even if you move at a slow pace at least you are moving and that is progress and progress is good. I remember when my family and I came to this country it was my aunt, three cousins, my uncle, sister, and my dad, in a small 1 bedroom, 1 bathroom apartment in Miami Beach and little by little there was progress it was a slow process but it was progress until one day everyone had their own home. Even in 2008 when the market crash we lost five homes in

Tampa and two properties here in Miami, but that didn't stop us, it doesn't matter because we continue to play the game to win.

When it comes to the game of life is good to know that success leaves foot prints if you follow the steps of successful people you are going to succeed sooner or later am glad I meet successful entrepreneurs in the online business some of them are millionaires, some of them are on their way to their first million including myself, millions of online entrepreneurs became millionaires using search engine optimization, social media and different ways to create online traffic, some of them are only making about $30,000 a month and for them this is a game and they love the game some are making millions with Facebook, with webinars, buying solo ads and other ways of marketing, I am glad I can follow those footsteps and I will love to encourage my family and friends and readers of this book to follow the same footsteps so they can work from home and so they can win in the game of money as well. I created an amazing course is like a game is called List Building Master Pro what this course does is educated people on how to build a list of buyers in the internet, people who are eager to buy your product online in any niche that you want, with this course you will be able to win the game of money and not only that but you are going to be able to play from home and make money from home just go and check it out go to www.ListBuildingMasterPro.com Remember success leaves foot print, this course that I have created is like a game the more you play it the more money you are going to make, the bigger your list of buyers the bigger your income, everybody needs buyers and the more the better play the money game to win not to lose.

Albert Einstein and Napoleon Hills Philosophy.

Einstein had say that everything is energy and that's all there is to it. Match the frequency of the reality you want and you cannot help but to get that reality. It can be no other way. This is NOT philosophy; this is physics.

This same concept could be apply to money. Think prosperity, think abundance, think wealth, think opportunity don't complain about money because if you do you are going to have less of it, you are going to create that reality, money is an idea, think big, think wealth be creative and soon you can have a few million dollars ideas and soon you can have the right people at the right time and the right team to help you build it. Napoleon Hills, the author of *Think and Grow Rich,* says that whatever the mind of man can conceive and believe, it can achieve. But you have to believe if you don't believe how can you achieve, you can't achieve If you don't believe the key here is to believe, grab that believe with energy and send it to the universe to God and match that frequency of that reality and you cannot help but to get what you want. It can be no other way. Believe in your dreams, think about your dreams all the time and the more you think about it the better.

Any idea, any plan or purpose may be placed in the mind through repetition of thought, think how can I create more wealth, think how can I become financially independent, repeat it in your mind over and over again and you will have the answer and opportunities will come to you.

Napoleon Hills also say that the starting point of all achievement is DESIRE. Is desire Keep this constantly in your mind. Because weak desire will brings weak results, just as a small fire makes a small amount of heat. Big desire create big results, and Einstein says that everything is energy why not put this burning desire with a lot of energy send it to God send it to the universe and soon you will see that that's all there is to it. It will match the frequency of the reality that you want and you cannot help but to get that reality. It can be no other way say Einstein and this is NOT philosophy this is physics.

The Bible says if you believe all things are possible, all things not a few things but all things. I understand that true wealth is in the mind true wealth is in the spirit. That's where it all begins but we have to believe.

Remember there is positive energy and there is negative energy, if you put in the world a negative energy you may get a negative situation, if you send that negative energy that may bring a bad day, a bad year, a bad habit, and everything else. Be aware of your thoughts; be aware of the way you think and use the power of faith and energy to get what you want, some people call it the law of attraction call it what you want but make it happen, create an energy of abundance, joy, wealth, happiness, love, peace of mind, happiness.

Success is a learnable skill, and you can learn how to become wealthy but if you don't believe you won't achieve.

CHAPTER 6

THE THREE PILLARS OF WEALTH

REAL ESTATE, STOCKS & BUSINESSES

The same way we have the pillars of good relationships and spirituality we have the pillars of wealth, in this chapter we are going to talk a little bit about all 3 pillars. Real Estate, Stocks, and Businesses.

Real Estate Investing

There are many ways to do creative real estate deals this are only a few examples.

Promissory notes Let me introduce you to the world of promissory notes what is a promissory note is a promise to pay a debt, it could be for a house, a boat, plane or car is a promise to pay if you don't pay they take away the collateral.

Am going to talk about three steps of promissory notes and is going to be based on real estate.

1. How to create a promissory note with a homeowner.
2. How to flip a promissory note to an Investor
3. How to buy it for your own investments to get high returns.

How To Create A Promissory Note.

Let's say you don't qualify to get a mortgage from the bank. You don't have a good credit score. Your job don't pay that much. But you want to buy a house and you see a nice house that you like and it says For Sale By Owner. You contact the owner he gets to like you and you like the property. The owner says that he is moving to another state next month and that he is desperate to sell. He needs to sell fast. He is selling it for $180,000 sometimes it takes a little bit of negotiation when it comes to do this. Sometimes not all the times it all depends how desperate is the owner to sell. the owner of the house needs to move by next month he is going to another state you can ask him if he is willing to finance the property tell him that you are willing to buy it this month. he may think about it he is not 100% sure so you contact him again next week and tell him that you have a nice check for him that you are willing to buy the house before the end of the month, tell him that you are going to give him 10% which is $18,000 that you are going to put that check on escrow he may get even more motivated because you are putting a check of $18,000 in an escrow account if he says yes, you just bought a house without going to the bank, he didn't check your financial or your credit score or the taxes. Remember all of this is negotiable maybe you can put less, if he say no offer him some interest like 6% maybe he gets even more motivated. If you don't have the $18,000 get a check from capital one or from another financial institution and put it as a down payment. But make sure you can make the payment on the house this is how you can create a promissory note. It is a promise to pay if you don't pay he will get the house back, let's say worst case scenario you cannot pay you have a few options you can rent the house and get some cash flow, or just sell it and make a profit. There is more creative things you can do but those two are the basic, I thought this techniques to a lot of people dozens of realtors and new investors I was surprise that there are realtors in the business for more than 10 years and they never heard about this, this means is lack of education but I don't blame them because most of the brokers don't know this either they don't teach it to them.

How to Flip a Promissory Note To An Investor.

When a homeowner finances a property most of the time in most counties this gets recorded and it goes to public records. That means that everybody could see it because is public records. Let's say you go to the public records in your county and you find a promissory note that you like. Let's say the owner is Pedro. He owns a promissory note of $162,000 at 6% interest that means that he is the owner of the house and he have finance the property to someone else. Let's say he finance the property to Mario that means that Mario owes $162,000 at 6% interest if Mario doesn't pay Pedro will keep the house. Mario is paying every month he pays on time and Pedro is happy because he is making good interest rate better than CD's lets' say is being 2 years and Pedro the owner of the Deed. The owner of the house receives a letter from Eduardo. Eduardo wants to offer Cash for his promissory note. Pedro calls Eduardo and he likes that Eduardo is offering cash in a flash. That means that Pedro is going to get cash in two weeks or less. Eduardo Offers Pedro $100,000 cash for his deed for the promissory note Pedro agrees. Eduardo will contact some investors to sell that promissory note. Eduardo haven't bought it yet but he have it under contract Eduardo is looking to flip this deal to an investor he contact Raymond the investor. Raymond wants to buy this good deal. He knows is a good investments. Raymond will pay $125,000 Cash. Raymond put the money in Escrow $125,000 Eduardo uses that money to pay Pedro the owner of the deed. The owner of the promissory note Eduardo pays Pedro $100,000 .

Eduardo just flipped a Promissory note without using his money and he put $25,000 in his pocket.

How to buy promissory note for your own investments to get high returns

This is just like the example 2, but instead of flipping it to Raymond, Eduardo will buy It for himself.

Eduardo will offer Pedro $100,000 cash, there is no mortgage in here it have to be cash, If Pedro says Yes, Pedro will sell it for $100,000 all they have to do is to go to a title company or escrow and do the paper work and that's it.

But Eduardo has to be smart enough to buy a good deal, because if you buy the promissory note you are buying the house and if the house have liens, or violations or maybe Pedro didn't pay the taxes, maybe the property needs a lot of repairs, maybe Mario is not paying the debt, or maybe there is no equity and you are buying something without equity. That's why it is important to do a title search if you are going to buy it for yourself and probably an appraiser to see the real value of the property, not the opinion of the owner but the real value of the property. But let's say there are no liens or nothing like that and there is equity.

Remember Mario owes $162,000 at 6% and the value of the property is $180,000 if Eduardo buys it $100,000 he just created a huge return on his pocket. Eduardo is going to get $162,000 at 6% for something that is worth $180,000 and if Mario doesn't pay Eduardo will keep the house and he only put $100,000.

Remember a Promissory Note is a Promise to pay if they don't pay you keep the property, this is a good business to learn but is not that easy it takes dedication and persistence a lot of wealthy people do this they can do this in residential and they can do this in commercial real estate, there are a lot of Millionaires and Billionaires that buys Promissory Note people like Robert Kiyosaki and her wife Kim, Robert Allen, and many more you can start small if you want you can start by flipping note, If you want to learn how to do this one of my mentor whose name is Russ Dalbey you probably have seen him on TV he buys this in abundance you can Google his name if you want too, I am not an affiliate of him or nothing like that, he will sell his books and CD's for about $35 or $45 that's a good price, but off course he may try to sell you training and more stuff for $1,000 or more you don't really need to pay more than $45 you will get more than enough training with that, remember this is a business just like any other business it may be challenge at the beginning but once you get it you get it. If you want to do something that is a lot easier go to www.TheOnlineBusiness.Info I teach people how to make money from home and how to be their own boss, I created 3 FREE Videos that will teach you how to make money from home and you will also get the FREE EBook via email.

Rehabs (Buy, Fix & Sell)

Buy, Fix and sell doesn't always mean buy, fix, and sell. A lot of investors have created this as a business a flipping business they buy, fix and flip right away and profit $20,000 minimum and some good properties can give you up $100,000 profit per property it all depends in the city, the economy and where the property is located, and what kind of offer you made on the property.

The best time to get into the flipping business is when there are a lot of foreclosure because it's cheap and investors like it when is cheap; they want to buy a property way below appraisal value.

The Three Types of Rehabs

Buy, Fix, Sell

Buy, Fix, Rent

Buy, Fix, Rent, Refinance Get the money out and buy more properties or pay off your private lender by getting a regular loan, you may have to wait at least six months to refinance it depends on the bank and the city or state you are buying. Once you have the property giving you some cash flow, it is a lot easier to go to the bank get a loan or refinance.

You can buy REO, Pre Foreclosure, Auctions, FSBO, Probate Home, Sheriff sale many ways to buy a house this are only a few. You always want to look for equity and look at all the expenses that you are going to have.

Expenses like Realtor commission, Title company for closing the deal, appraiser to know the appraise value of the property you must know the value after is repair, Money borrow for the deal the fees and the interest rate, contractors labor and money to back you up for a few months just in case something goes wrong.

How are you buying are you using your own money, private money, hard money. Are you getting a mortgage, business partner money, personal loan, business loan at what interest, you have to have that in consideration, you must know your numbers.

If you want to invest with Alan go to www.InvestingWithAlan.com we buy fix and sell properties and I am also a private lender that lend money to other investor, when we lend money the investor have to buy a property with equity and they have to put $35% down and then we lend him or her the money only if he qualify, only if he is an experience investor and have a good track record if not we will reject him. Invest with Alan and get 7% to 9% interest on your money, good ROI great return, invest with Alan your money will always be protected and secured by real estate, a lot of equity and you will always have collateral go to www.InvestingWithAlan.com **to watch the videos.** Let's get to know each other let's talk and if we are a good match we move forward.

Tax Deed and Tax Liens

What is a tax lien certificate? When someone doesn't pay the taxes on the property, it becomes a tax lien. But it doesn't become a tax lien right away. Let me give you an example:

Let's say Maria she is the owner of a property and she forgot to pay her taxes the county is going to send the owner Maria letters saying that she needs to pay the taxes on her property the county is going to send her letter many times for a few months maybe up to a year or two is she doesn't pay is going to build up that debt on taxes let's say she owe $3,222 for 2015 and she didn't pay and now she is also owe for 2016 that is an extra $3,556 the county is going to harass Maria telling her that she needs to pay her taxes for the property, if Maria doesn't pay they are going to sell it to an investor.

Now Maria owes taxes for 2015 & 2016, which is $3,222 + $3,556 = $6,778 total. The county is selling this debt that Maria owes, now Maria is going to have to pay the debt plus high interest that is bad news for Maria. but for the investor is good news because he is secured and protected by the government knowing that he is going to get paid with high interest. Here in FL the Tax Lien Certificate starts at 18% each state is different some are higher some are lower. well the county is selling the Tax Lien Certificate that Maria owes to the highest bidder let's say they are selling her debt for 2015 & 2016 and Eduardo comes along he is an investor and he starts bidding on the debt that Maria have on the taxes. the bidding starts at 18% the bidding will go down not up 17% - 16% - 15% - 14.5% - 14% - 13%- 12.5% - 12% Sold To Eduardo the investor just bought a tax lien certificate at 12% Now Maria have to pay Eduardo the taxes she owe for 2015 & 2016 at 12%.

Every state is different some states you can get high interest as much as 36% and in some as low as 8% but the main point of this is that anyone can come and buy tax lien certificate this could be you or anyone who wants to buy it. And this is guaranteed to get your money back because the government will force Maria to pay. Or you will get the deed just wait for the redemption period to expire. After that you only have to wait about 180 days and apply for the deed and then the property will be yours. Each state is different but is the same concept.

Tax Deed

A Tax Deed is the actual property without any mortgage payment, when you are buying a Tax Deed you are buying the property that is free and clear and this is also an auction but every county is different, let's say the sale of this property starts at $6,778 and the appraisal value of the property is $110,000 and the last bidding price goes up to $54,000 and the winner bidder was Eduardo. Once Eduardo buys this house he can do whatever he wants with it, he can sell it, rent it , move in to the property, let's say he decide to sell it fast in 30 days or less Eduardo sells it for $88,000 he just profit $34,000 in one deal.

Imagine if he can just do 8 to 20 deals like this every year and he only did it part time. well this could happen to anyone if you want to invest with Alan go to www.InvestingWithAlan.com my team and I are looking to raise capital to invest in Tax Deed if you want to invest you have the opportunity to make big money with us. You will also have collateral on the properties and get a nice interest rate we are looking to raise between 5 to 20 million every year I have an entire team that buys properties. Invest with Alan and get huge ROI amazing return. All the properties we get have 40% to 50% equity and more. Your investment will always be secured by real estate always. A good asset with a lot of equity or if you are looking to learn how to do this we do a Free Seminar 1 day training where you can learn how to invest in Tax Deed & Tax Lien Certificate go to www.AlanKeysToSuccess.com and get your Free Bonus Training. There should be a link for the FREE EVENT.

If you want to invest with Alan go to www.InvestingWithAlan.com In Tax Deed.

Example: Our Highest Bid is up to 55% of the appraise value, to protect the investor and to protect everyone and to create a win-win for everyone. Before you invest with Alan you need to get approved we need to get to know you first you need to get to know us, if we both agree we move forward.

Appraised Value	$150,000	$220,000	$180,000
Highest Bid 55%	$82,500	$121,000	$99,000

We are always looking to buy properties with equity that means that your investment is always secured.

There are many ways to do creative real estate over 35 techniques on Real Estate investing I just went over a few in this chapter there is residential and commercial real estate, seller finance, lease option, Master lease option, triple Net, subject too, wrap around mortgage, contract for deed, etc…. the idea is to get the right education to make some smart financial decisions or partner with someone that can make those smart financial decisions.

Stocks

Stocks are pieces of the company, which are called shares—pieces of ownership of the company that any person can buy.

When it comes to stock, we have long-term stocks and we have short-term stocks.

The difference is that long-term stock holders or long-term stock investors buy and hold for years to come it could be 3 years to 40 years or more.

Short-term stocks or day traders they buy today and they sell it 45 minutes later or they sell it 8 hours later is only for a short period of time.

When it comes to stock you want to buy low and sell high, but there are also other techniques that you can use like options, short selling it means that you can make money whether the market goes up, down or sideways, but if you are NOT using options or shortselling you are only making money when the market goes up.

When it comes to stocks, there are over 40,000 stocks to choose from and that could be very overwhelm that's why is very important to get educated, investors that invest long term believe in the product of the company and the leadership that is behind it, if you want to do long term stocks you may want to see the financial of that company and the track record that it haves, you can own shares of Coca Cola, Wells Fargo buying shares of the company means that you are part owner of the company a small part and that is an asset and that is what you want in your portfolio and why did I say Coca Cola and Wells Fargo well for many reason Warren Buffet the best stock investor in the world owns shares of Coca Cola & Wells Fargo and this are company that being around even before my grandfather was born and even when the market goes down and crashes people still buy Coca Cola and Wells Fargo are buying other banks that are not that strong. I remember when Wells Fargo bought Wachovia I used to have Wachovia and that's what you need to invest and buy shares of strong companies that are going to be around here in 30 years and more warren buffet knows this companies are going to be here in 30 years and more that's why he buys shares of the company and when he buys he buys a lot.

You always want to see the financials of the companies if you are going to do long term you want to know the results now and how this company has being doing in the past 3 years - 10 years – 30 years -50 years. If you like the numbers and the percentages this companies are giving percentage wise, maybe you can make a decision on investing on them. Always do your due diligence, read the chart understand it talk to a few good Financial Advisor or Stock Brokers talk to them and get more information. You can also become a stock trader or option trader you will manage your own stocks instead of having a broker manage it for you, you will be able to buy and sell stocks in the short term and make a killing instead of waiting for the long term but there is some risk 70% of people that do this lose money the other 30% are killing it because they have the education, they are making millions, there is a risk and there is a reward on doing this. The idea is to start small and once you get good at it then you go big and don't put all your money in one basket either. I myself a student of this because I want to master this I just don't want to be in the 30% but I want to be the best at doing this, I want to be in the top 1 percent.

Even though I know about this topic and strategies like Options, short am still getting educated and that's what you want to do as well, is funny because am going to an event the same week this book is getting published. I will continue to go to more events because I want to learn more and maybe you should do the same. Don't be average; if you are average you are going to get average results and you don't want that decide to be in the top 1 percent. Get the knowledge, invest in your education is going to be one of the best decisions you have made. When it comes to trading stocks or doing Forex don't ask your stock broker for advice 80% of them all they do is long term stocks, bonds, mutual funds, index funds, bonds, IRA, & 401k a lot of them think trading stocks is risky, but like I say there is a risk and there is a reward and the reward could be really big IF you know what you doing that's why getting the knowledge and education is very important. Sometimes it seems like am contradicting myself because I say listen to the brokers and then I say don't listen to them, but read again if you have to if you are listening on audio, listen to it again.

Get educated when it comes to doing options and shorts if you do that you are going to be able to double and triple your money in no time learn how to read the charts and don't depend on the broker learn how to make money in a bullish market and a bearish market, bullish is when the market is going up and bearish is when the market is going down and you can make money in both markets. This is one of the secrets of the rich, they don't depend on the broker instead they created their own wealth.

Taking Your Business Public

The average person could also take his business public if they have a business but this takes more dedication, discipline it takes entrepreneur skills, knowledge and a good business plan to do this lets say Trouble Clothing line, wants to be big like Nike, Tommy Hilfiger, and Adidas. He may be able to do that if he have investors investing in his company let's say he takes 10 investors and each invest $100,000 a total of one million and within 5 years Trouble Clothing line reach ten million the investors will be happy and the owner of Trouble clothing line as well, creating a win-win for everyone and he may even have thousands of investors investing in his corporation and that could be the beginning of a successful journey.

The same could be with someone that is running a wholesale distribution business or any business let's say Manolo meat Corporation distribute wholesale meet to local restaurants, but if he sell shares of his company and decide to grow he may end up doing all around FL or all around the USA. But like I say this takes discipline, skills, and preparation and probably working with someone that knows how to take a company public and then you can sell shares of your company that's how many companies when from being little to be big companies like Kmart, Ford, Walmart, Nike, Costco etc.

Forex

Forex means Foreign Exchange; you are exchanging currency is the wealth of different countries. It is not like stocks that you own shares of a business this is exchange of currency. There are three important markets that any forex professional knows:

The Asian market it opens at 5 am.

The USA market opens at 8 am.

European market open at 2am.

The Foreign Exchange trades are an estimated of $5.3 Trillion daily, which means traders are buying and selling one currency against another and that also means that there is a lot of opportunity for any person that wants to get involve.

The good thing about this is that there are three levels of trading: Micro lots, Mini lots, and the Standard. The Micro lots you can start trading with as little as less as $100 or less your returns are going to be very little, the mini lot you can trade in average between $100 to $999 , the standard you can trade anything that is over 1 thousand that's where I got started.

You can also start with no money with paper trading; if you don't put any money you are not going to get any profit, paper trading is only practicing you don't make any money there because you didn't put any money. Is good if you just want to learn and practice.

In Forex, you can trade when the market is going up or down if you have your strategies and you can trade for a few minutes or for a few hours if you want. And not only that but doing forex will give you 10, 20, 30 times more than any mutual fund or index fund. Maybe you should consider to learn how to do Forex. I myself am still taking classes about this.

Am going to talk about Mutual Fund and Index Funds probably in the next page this is what most financial advisors will recommend you to do, there is nothing wrong with that is not as good as Forex or doing option trading. Mutual Fund and Index Funds are still assets but you have to leave it there for the long-term.

Remember the rule of 72, there are stock traders and forex traders that understand option and shorten that are making between 50% to 300% return on their money every single year. Let's say we only make 72% a year consistent, how long would it take for our money to double. 72 ÷ 72% = 1 year, that's why you want to be in the top 30% of the successful traders that know how to trade. If you do this you will be successful, your goal should be to be in the top 5% or 1% of successful traders.

Example:

Years	72%
1	$10,000
2	$20,000
3	$40,000
4	$80,000
5	$160,000
6	$320,000
7	$640,000
8	$1,280,000
9	$2,560,000
10	$5,120,000
11	$10,240,000
12	$20,480,000

13	$40,960,000
14	$81,920,000
15	$163,840,000

Am I saying that you are going to get those results? No. You may get more, or you may get less; this was just an example.

Karen Bruton, a regular CPA, started trading full time in 2007. In about 3 or 4 years, she made over $40 Million doing options and shorts this was about the time the market crash and then she made over $200 Million in total and there is thousands of people having the same success just like hers.

Bruce Kovner used to be a taxi driver for many years and now he is a billionaire making about $800 Million a year. He is now a hedge fund manager in Wall Street.

Jeffrey Epstein was a school teacher and now he is a billionaire because he learned how to trade in the stock market, making over $600 million a year. That's over a million dollars a day.

For most middle class or poor people, they don't think this is possible; that's the reason it will never happen to them. But if you read Trader magazine, Fortune Magazine, or any other success magazines, this things are normal its happening every single day, it happens all the time, but most people that don't believe all they do is watch TV, listen to the radio and watch the bad news on TV, and then they are complaining thinking that everything is bad, they think is hard or that it is impossible to become wealthy.

Mutual Funds

This is a group of investors putting their money together to buy stocks, shares of a company, and bonds or in some cases a combination of both.

I am going to tell you the good and the bad of mutual funds a lot of mutual funds can give you a return of 5% to 10% and the fees are about 2% to 3 % so you do your math, also take in consideration inflation 2% to 3% every year. Here in the united states we have ups and down in the economy an average of 2 or 3 crashes in 30 years now let's talk how this is manage. The fund is managed by a professional fund manager who manages the portfolio. Mutual Fund investments are subject to the market going up or down, just like everything in the world there is always risk even driving to work could be risky but if you leave your money for the long-term, the risk is minimum. If you only want to put it there for 2 years to 5 years, the risk may be higher it all depends when are you buying when the market is going up or down. Just like real estate you can buy a house but the value may go up or down, if you are investing in mutual funds for the long-term 10 to 30 years or longer the chances of making money is greater just like stocks, remember Mutual Funds is a pool of a lot of companies a lot of stocks or a combination of stocks and bonds.

Mutual Funds are considered an asset and you want an assets in your portfolio. If you get some mutual funds look for something that is 8.5% to 11% you may not get a 11% but just look for it ask brokers, some mutual funds, stocks double and triple in value in the long term, having a mutual fund is better than having your money in CDs.

You may want to talk to a few bankers 3 or more or a few stock brokers or money managers and ask to see how that mutual fund is being doing in the past 3 years – 10 years – 30 years and 50 years and see what percentage that mutual fund is giving. But remember always ask to see full disclosure of brokers fee, annual fees and any other fees that may come with it and how often do they charge those fees, you want 100% full disclosure before you make an agreement if you like it go for it.

You can become an investor with $1,000; in some cases, you can even put less. The best way to learn this is to ask questions, ASK ASK ASK to those financial advisors just go to your bank and ask you don't have to buy nothing yet is not an obligation but do get the information and the sooner you get the information the better, if you don't want to be an average investor you can learn how to trade stocks you may do 10 or 20 times better than having a few mutual funds in your portfolio for the long term.

Index Funds

This is a group of stocks known as the market index. They have low fees, less than mutual funds and is track by software and computer is not track by a group of managers that's why you can save money. In Index Funds, you will have lower cost and lower fees; it means more money for you. As an example the S & P 500 is track by software, is track by the same results that it have, it doesn't try to beat the market, but it tracks the market index the way it is. That's why Index Funds have done better than actively managed funds over time.

BUSINESSES

The Online Business

The internet has made millions of millionaires all around the world and if you choose to make a fortune in the internet, you can do that, if you make less than $10,000 a month in the internet it means that you need to learn how to make money in the internet if you are making an average of $10,000 a month in the internet you still need to learn a lot more. One of my friends and mentors is making about 10 Million a year in the internet and he still wants to learn a lot more. He listens to webinars, he continues to buy other people's products and this is a guy who makes 10 million a year. I also have other friends or people I have met that make less than $50,000 a year but they don't want to go to the event;

they don't want to listen to the webinar and when I tell them that there is a seminar, they say no thank you. I already know that that's what they say, is sad but that's the reality, if you want to be successful, you have to be open to learn.

The first step to make money in the internet is to learn how to do it; once you have the mindset this could set you free financially it may take a few months for you to get it and to change your old habits but once you get it you get it.

This is no longer the industrial age things change and if you don't change with things you are going to be left behind, the industrial age is old school, this is not the 80's or 90 or 2001 this is the new age the informational age, did you know that there is over 68 Billion dollar worth of information being sold in the internet every year, and the number continues to grow, all of this products have being sold in Facebook, YouTube, Google, Yahoo, Pinterest, Twitter, D-linked, EBay, Forum sites, Blogger and thousands of other websites.

How much money did you made in Facebook last week or in YouTube? If you are making less than $15,000 a month, you have to learn how to make money in the internet, even if you are making $150,000 a month you should continue to learn or you will stay behind, look at my friend he makes about 10 million a year and he continues to learn, he continues with his education.

Remember this is not the 80s or 90s or the beginning of 2001 anymore. The old techniques were good on those days, but the game has change and if you are not aware of that and if you are not willing to change, you are going to lose in the game. Go get the education; there is still time to learn.

I wish I could teach you everything I know about becoming an Online Entrepreneur in this chapter, but it will take me about 2 or 3 books just to do that. All I can say is that you can sell online products without having to buy them, and without having to ship anything, without talking to any customer, without any inventory or nothing like that and the best part is that you can do this from home you don't have to get a lease in an office building or rent a location in a shopping center .

If you want to become an online entrepreneur, I created 3 FREE videos that will teach you how to do that from home, the first video will show you how to choose your product without having to pay for it, there are millions of products you can choose some of the product are about.

- Technology
- Education
- Dating
- Parenting
- Business
- Finance
- Investments
- Traveling
- Health
- Spirituality
- Sports and many more.

I will show you how to do that in the first FREE Video. The second Video is how to build a list of buyers that will buy your product all the time and the third video is a surprise. Just go to www.TheOnlineBusiness.Info put your name and email and I will send it to your email right away, you don't have to pay anything is FREE.

Get the information, get the education, get the 3 FREE Videos I made for you, this is a gift just for getting this book.

Once you learn these techniques, you will be ready to make money from home.

The Market Place

Whether you make $20,000 a year or $20,000,000 a year, you are getting pay according to your contribution in the market place, the more you give the more you will receive when it comes to economics you have a price tag some people have a price tag of minimum wage or $9 - $10 an hour and others have a price tag of $1,000 an hour and more, whether is $20,000 a year or $20,000,000 a year according to economics to the market place you have a price tag, but according to God you are priceless. Meanwhile you are here on earth you are going to get paid according to your contribution, the idea is to contribute get paid save that money and invest, remember this always: save to invest and spend less than you earn.

When it comes to personal finance basics, it is important to choose cleverly when and how to invest your savings. Put your money to work earning high interest don't put your money on CD's; instead do what I have shown you in this book. There are difference places where you can put your money and get higher return. If anything, you can put it on a house with equity, a duplex put it in a four-plex with FHA that is 3.5% down or a 10 unit apartment, if you have enough savings or higher you can also lend it out and get high interest rate there are many places where you can get 6% to 25%, or just pay of your mortgage which is a good idea.

Giving Value to the Marketplace

The more value you give to the marketplace the more wealth you are going to create, focus on giving your value to the market place. Because the market place is going to make you wealthy, you will get paid in direct proportion to the value you deliver according to the marketplace, let me give you an example let's say you own a distribution company and you deliver food to only 30 restaurants, but your competitor is delivering food to 1,000 restaurants who do you think is going to create more wealth, I think you know the answer already and yes knowing your expenses and income is very important and many other aspects of the business as well. What about the company that delivers cars from one state to another? ABC company is delivering 10 cars a month from Florida to Texas, am sure they will make a good income but the company XYZ is delivering 100 cars a month from Florida to Texas is the same process but one is giving more to the market place and that's why is making 10 times more.

Knowing the Demand and Supply is important before getting into any business venture, the same as knowing the quality and quantity.

Let me give you an example of quantity. An attorney makes good money, good income but do you think an attorney can handle 100 new clients a week, every week I don't think he will be able to handle it, but an online entrepreneur can make 100 sales a week and he can do that from home every single week as long he have internet connection and he will be able to do it part time instead of full time as long as he has a system. If the system is good IT CAN WORK WITHOUT HIM 24hours a day, 7 days a week, 365 days in a year. And he can sell a product that can produce a profit of $100 to $1,000 without a problem as long as there is a demand and the market place wants it and this doesn't include the funnel the upsell or down sell, is also a huge leverage because he doesn't even have to talk to any customer, or have any inventory.

I am not saying one is better than the other is all about your passion what you like and what you love, my mom was a school teacher for more than 20 years and she loved it; my dad was a psychologist for many years and he enjoy it; they did it because they love what they do, my path is not to be a school teacher or to be a phycology but I do study the psychology of wealth creation and I do like to apply it and teach it. Choose your passion choose your path and go in that direction, but you may want to consider becoming an online entrepreneur as well at least part time. In the long run it will pay off big time.

If you want wealth, you have to think wealth, and what better way than the internet to position yourself for wealth. Start giving something your product or service and in return you will get that wealth.

Technology is changing the game and is changing quickly and if you are not going with the changes that are around you, you will have missed a lot of opportunities and a lot of money. A lot of people are becoming rich by creating new software, Apps, creating online businesses and different ways of improving technology, just with the internet alone regular people just like you and I are becoming millionaires every minute of every hour and this is happening every single day, a lot of entrepreneurs are making millions just with Facebook, same as Google and Pinterest and many other websites. Be aware with the changes around you and take advantage of them, you may have to make some changes, remember success is a learnable skill. That's why the past does not equal the future.

Getting Interest on your Money

This is another effective way to get high interest in your money if you want to make an average of 6% to 11%. There are a lot of places you can go to lend your money. You can lend it to me I will always give you collateral real estate, a lot of equity so you won't have any risk, but if you don't want to do that or you don't have enough money you can go to:

www.lendingclub.com   or   www.lendingtree.com

There are many companies you can lend your money, but I like these two because I used to borrow money from them but now I lend them money. I like them because they are very ethical, and you can start with very little money, but there is one thing they won't give you collateral or any guarantee. I am not an affiliate of them, you can go to their website, call them, look at the investing page in their website and ask them questions. This would be between you and them—100% your risk.

If you want to have something secured with equity if you want to invest in a real asset just go to www.InvestingWithAlan.com we can do some Rehabs, Tax Deed or Tax Lien or invest in Commercial Real Estate, but first we need to talk and get to know each other let's see if you and I are a good match to do business together.

CHAPTER 7

PROTECT YOURSELF AND PROTECT YOUR ASSETS

Get Insurance

There are all kinds of insurance, insurance for your properties, businesses, life insurance, disability insurance, health insurance, car insurance, Insurance for the valuable things that you have in your house, even insurance for stocks for your investments, well in reality is like an insurance for your stocks, you may not need all the insurance there are out there, you don't need a home insurance if you don't have a house, you may not need life insurance if you are single, no kids no family or any relative, but if you have assets if you have businesses you should protect yourself.

As much as we hope that emergencies won't happen, we all know that they do. What insurance does is buy peace of mind; nobody wants something bad to happen, to their business or home, and we hope we never use it. What if a love one doesn't have health insurance and is involved in a life and death situation? Severe weather could flood your basement or crack your pipes and you don't have the right insurance. What if your business burns down or you get sued and you are not protected? Any of these emergencies can be expensive, and we all hope this doesn't happen but sometimes things do happen. So why not be prepared rather than potentially become another victim or suffer a pain of an emergency. This is one important aspect of your finances that you need to consider. You've worked hard to build a firm financial footing for you and your family, so it needs to be protected. Accidents and disasters can and do happen and if you aren't efficiently insured it could leave you in financial disaster. Good quality insurance can protect your life, it can protect your assets, your ability to earn income, and to keep a roof over your head. The most important insurance you can get are the ones that can protects your assets as well as life insurance, disability insurance, health insurance.

Life Insurance.

I am not an Insurance agent, but you definitely want to talk to a few of them. Always compare prices talk to four, five, or more. A lot of this firms can insure you and your family for half a million or a million just in case you pass away. Nobody wants this to happen but if it does your wife and kids will have money after your dead, you don't want to leave them with debt. Not everyone needs Life Insurance but if you have a family and they depend on you, you better have Life insurance. Like I say before there are all type of insurance but life Insurance is a must if you have family depend on you.

Home Insurance.

Even if your house is paid off, make sure you have a good insurance that can cover your house just in case an emergency happens, emergencies like hurricane, flood etc....

Protect your Investments

There are all kinds of insurance, you can protect your stocks your investments so you don't lose money like I say before is like an insurance for your stocks, but you have to learn how to do it by becoming an option trader.

I could probably tell you that more than 90% of people that invest in stocks don't know that; that's why they are always losing money. I remember the time I was studying to become a stock broker. To work for a financial institution, all I had to do is take the exam and pass it. But I was asking myself what are they teaching me? It was the opposite of what successful stock traders do; it was totally different approach of Warren Buffet way to invest, it was all about financial law that will protect the company the firm, benefit for the firms, and all the hiding fees that the government and the financial institution will take from the people, it wasn't even teaching me the right material. Everything was laws and ways to protect the big firms, and myself so I don't lose the license.

They didn't teach anything about stocks, even when they were talking about options, futures, and short selling it was totally different than the way successful investors invest. Let me be honest with you; all these stock brokers make a commission just to sell you something, whether is good or bad. They make a commission when they do a transaction, some of them they don't even know what they are selling because they don't have the expertise. This is a joke they are playing with other people money just to get a commission; if that stock is so good, ask them if they are investing in that stock. Almost all of them will say no and they only talk about long-term stocks and in a lot of financial firms like banks the broker is not allowed to advice the clients when it comes to options, futures or shorts what if you want to rent your stock you probably won't be able to do that with a bank either, protect your assets and get some financial education it will help you in the long run, that's one of the reason I didn't become a stock broker.

Asset Protection

Creating your wealth is one thing, but protecting it is the most important thing. I am not an attorney; my best recommendation to you is to speak to a few that have enough experience in Asset Protection. Find someone with at least five years of experience. Find the best one, you always want the best one in your team.

You don't need to be rich to protect your assets. The rich are no longer the only lawsuit target, middle class and the poor are also being sued, a lot of people are being sued for no reason. If you have any assets now, you need protection, you don't want to be sued and then you lose everything you have built for years, you want to protect your investments, businesses, you want to protect yourself from all types of lawsuit and from different situations, you want to protect yourself from a divorce even before you get married. Find out the best way to leave a good inheritance just in case something happens to you, ask how to avoid probate, how to patent your ideas or your creations just like the Wright brothers have paten their projects for their first flying planes, just like the inventor Philo Farnsworth paten television even thou he was bitten down by his competitor David Sarnoff and David Sarnoff took all the glory and fame, according to the United States government was Philo Farnsworth the inventor of electronic television, he couldn't sell it or create a business out of it, but he was the creator and the inventor.

Protect your ideas patent them, you don't want someone like Mark Zuckerberg to steal your ideas and made a fortune out of it just like he did with the twin brothers and his friend that are known for co-founding Harvard Connection and later renamed ConnectU. They wanted to create a successful social website like facebook but they couldn't but Mark Zuckerberg did.

When it comes to building your wealth, an attorney is a key factor to have in your team. If you don't have anything right now to protect don't worry but if you do this is something you want to consider.

Meet with a few corporate attorneys, attorneys that focus on Asset Protection, you may get a free consultation just go and ask, they want your service if is worth it go give them a job, you may want to ask the attorney what corporation would be better for your company, it all depends on the vision and plan of the company that's what he is going to tell you, so ask yourself what is your vision what's your plan.

If you want to do real estate investing, you want to have a real estate attorney in your team. They can help you with the contracts, and also to avoid a lot of headaches like law sues and all the legal papers.

Create a Huge Passive Income For Your Retirement

Financial Freedom is when your Passive Income is greater than your expenses, that's financial freedom, Passive Income is money that comes without you having to work.

Real Estate can do that; businesses will do that; the internet can do that as well. Learning how to invest could be the best thing you can do financially especially if you are thinking for retirement.

I personally don't want to depend on the government in the 401k or IRA. I rather have control of my money than having the government control my money and I don't know what is going to happen in 30 years from now. I personally don't have a 401k or IRA. I rather create my fortune now while I am still young. If I have no choice I probably put some money there when am 35 or 40 years old.

If you have money in an IRA, make sure you have some Index Mutual Funds as well. You can use the money that is in your IRA for investments purpose to buy bonds, mutual funds or Index Mutual funds and get some small interest of 6% to 10% in average, minus brokers commission it will be a little bit less. It is your choice.

If your employer is matching you to put money in your retirement, it is a good idea to put more money there, the more the better even if they match you with 20% or 40% Free money is Free money, my friend. I myself don't have this. I am not against it either I just have a different believe my intention and purpose is to create wealth now and to help my love ones now, don't get me wrong is a good idea and a good plan for retirement if you want to be secured and stable, I believe we all should be secured and stable but is better if you create wealth right now. Tax lien certificates can give you some amazing return same as promissory notes or trading the stock market or forex. Remember that Colonel Sanders started his business at the age of 66 he is the founder of KFC. If he can do it, you can do it—anybody can do it.

Final Word

There is going to be a learning curve when it comes to managing your finances and creating wealth. The sooner you start, the better is going to be for you. Creating wealth is a skill you can acquire whether in real estate investing, businesses, or stocks.

More importantly, don't be afraid to make mistakes. Learn from your mistake and keep moving forward. However, keep your eyes on your financial goals as you work toward it. Keep your eyes in the future; don't look at the left, don't look at the right. Just put your eyes on the prize in your financial goals. Create a plan a financial plan. If you don't have one you may fail financially and you don't want that all the wealthy people I have met they all have a good financial plan and they execute their plan.

One of my mentors thought me three key factor that made him extremely successful. I wish I would have learned this 10 years ago.

1- **Knowledge:** Get the knowledge; learn as much as you can about your business and how to be financially free. Get educated, you can always improve your skills whether is in marketing, selling, negotiating, real estate, stocks, Forex, creative finance, leadership, managing, etc. You can always be more, have more and do more because you can always learn more. Get the knowledge—that's where it all begins. Improve your financial IQ

2- **Strategies:** Develop creative ways to move ahead, develop a creative mindset. What strategies are you going to use to raise money, to buy or sell real estate, to buy or sell businesses, or to start a business? What are your exit strategies? You may have to get ideas form different people, find ways to be more creative, be a problem solver be bigger than the problem or challenge. Look at things from different points of view or from different perspectives, choose your best strategies A – B – C. Look at opportunities instead of problems. Search and ask for better ideas for better understanding and for better results.

3- **Execute:** You can be the smartest person in the world; you can have all the knowledge you want, but if you don't take action, nothing is going to happen. If you have to start small, at least start move forward. Don't stop don't quit, you are three feet from gold. Execute and finish the task, start and finish all the time, don't do it half way, success is doing it all the way. Action is the key to greatness, NO action no greatness if you want greatness you have to execute. Not only day dream but to put your dreams into action.

I could talk a lot more about these three key factors for success, but I think you get the point.

True wealth is not only material wealth, but also spiritual wealth remember that and don't ever forget it while you are creating your material wealth.

Gandhi said that it is health that is real wealth and not pieces of gold and silver. Look at Steve Jobs; he had all the money most people will wish for, but he didn't have the health he wanted.

Be grateful if you have health. Be grateful for what you have; be grateful for your loves ones, have that attitude of gratitude, always be thankful, and ask God for healing, wisdom, and truth. The truth is that the best things in life are free like love, joy, happiness, remember the kingdom of God is within you, and that is priceless.

You can have anything you want if you put your mind to it. You may have to search it at first, but if you search you will find everything you need is within your reach is near you. The right knowledge and information can be closer than you think; it may be in the library, maybe in Google, or YouTube search for good ideas, ideas of wealth, ideas of prosperity, ideas that can make you and your business better, read the books get the knowledge, search and ask for wisdom. I hope this book was helpful for you. If you have enjoy it and like it tell a friend to get a copy of this book or a few for him and his friends, family members or staff. Remember believe in yourself; believe in abundance my friend, thank you for reading this book and sharing it with others, If you have like it please put a nice comment on the site that you bought it from or a 5 stars it only takes a minute you are blessed.

About The Author

Alan Eduardo Ortega is a Real Estate Investor, Option Trader in Stocks, Trading Forex, and a Online Entrepreneur. In 2008 I started working in a Mortgage Company and 7 months later the company when out of business, many banks and mortgage companies when out of business because of the economy crash that's when I decided to learn as much as I possible can about real estate investing, businesses and all type of investments and my journey started since. In 2008 I began studying and doing businesses, investments and finances. I have study in a technical School in business computer, went to Trump University for 3 years, Enlighten Wealth Institute, Market Traders Institute, and continue with my education with many wealth institute like Millionaire Mind Intensive, High Traffic Academy and plenty more. I am looking to raise millions in capital for big projects, doing big syndications for Residential and Commercial Real Estate.

I have done plenty of deals with my partners, if you want to be part of my team you can go to www.AlanEduardo.com or www.InvestingWithAlan.com .

Alan Eduardo is also in the field of Personal Development, Self-Motivation, Spirituality and the power of Healing. In 2017 I will come up with my second book in the field of Personal Development and will do training events and seminars to educated and train the people that needs it the most. My Goal will always be to help and serve as many people as I possibly can.

www.TheOnlineBusiness.info

Get your **FREE Training**, I have created 3 powerful videos that teaches anyone on how to **make money from home**, Go to this site and watch the **3 FREE videos** I made for you and you will get your **Free E-Book** as well, making money from home is easy once you get it. All you have to do is put your name and email and you will be able to watch the **Free videos**, this videos will show you and teach you **how to make money from home and be your own boss**. Becoming an Online Entrepreneur is one of the best choices anyone can make. If you are looking to take advantage of your Entrepreneur spirit and created wealth from home go to www.TheOnlineBusiness.info and take advantage of your **Free training course**, this is my **Free gift** to you for getting this book.

www.ListBuildingMasterPro.com

List Building Master Pro is perfect for anyone who wants to start a successful online Business and create a big list of buyers that are ready and eager to buy your product. A lot of big companies understand this philosophy of List Building.

So who can do this and Who is this for This is for anyone who wants to make money from home even if you are a experience Internet Marketers, Network Marketers, or Any Online Entrepreneur, If you want to **make a lot of money from home,** If you want to get out of the rat race, I can help you, 88% of **Online Entrepreneurs** are struggling to make it happen, but you are not going to be one of them you are going to be able to **print your own wealth** once you learn this **Easy - Simple System.** Just go to www.ListBuildingMasterPro.com Get empower get ready to be a master at list building, building a list of buyers and be ready to make money from home.

www.AlanStopsForeclosure.com

Don't let the bank take your home, If you or anyone you know is behind on their mortgage payments or facing foreclosure, please help them tell them to go to www.AlanStopsForeclosure.com I am a foreclosure expert, I can stop a foreclosure and I CAN help you keep your home. There are basic principles and strategies to provide you and to insure you success!

Let go of the fear of losing your home and act on the faith that it can remain yours. If you want to sell it you can also contact me at the website and I will make you an offer in 72 hours or less. It don't matter if there are liens, violations, behind on payments, have two mortgages, needs repair I can help you stop foreclosure or make an offer in your house.

That's for every type of mortgage loan, whether prime rate loans, sub-prime loans or FHA loans and for military families. I will negotiate with your bank and create a win win situation contact Alan Eduardo at www.AlanStopsForeclosure.com don't wait until is to late lets solve the problem fast.

www.TheBookOnPersonalFinance.com

Here is where you can get my book Personal Finance and Wealth Creation Secrets, am also going to create some Videos, CDs, training and seminars about wealth creation, some amazing tips in Business, Investing, tips in the three pillars of wealth Real Estate Investing, Stocks & Forex, and Business.

When I talk about business I focus on Online Business without any inventory, without having to buy or getting a lease to open the doors, I would rather sell 24/7 all around the world. Let the internet and website make money this is what I teach my clients, is easier and faster. In this website I will put some FREE Videos and training as well about powerful leverage and creative ways to make money.

www.AlanKeysToSuccess.com

Visit my site you will be able to see my book Personal Finance and Wealth Creation Secrets and some small booklets I have of Goal Setting, Leadership and my future books will be in this site as well. You will be able to see some other sites that I have or websites that I be creating.

I will also put some FREE VIDEOS and training different than other videos and trainings.

Many products that I will create will be in this site.

www.InvestingWithAlan.com

If you want to invest your money and have some good return of 6% to 10% secured by real estate go to www.InvestingWithAlan.com all the properties will have equity that means that is way below appraise value, you will be secured by real estate, you will have a real estate attorney protecting you and myself, your name will be in the promissory note, if we don't pay you, you keep an asset.

My main focus are only 4 powerful investments. I will focus on

1 - Buying, Fixing and Selling,

2 - Tax Deed & Tax lien certificates.

3 - You can become a private lender with Alan we can lend the money secured by Real Estate and get some huge interest rate.

4 - Buying Commercial Real Estate big properties 40 unit apartment, 100 unit apartment, 200 unit apartment we can do a big syndication. I can do some creative real estate deals for a small down payment like seller finance, Master Lease Option, Equity partnership, a mix of private lending and seller finance etc....

We will always have a Real Estate Attorney doing all the contracts and paper work that will be for our protection.

The End

If you liked the book please recommend it, let's change some lives together. If you have liked it give me a good review in the website that you bought it.

Thank you for purchasing this book and for reading it, I hope you liked it a lot and learned a lot.